AS A SEAL UPON YOUR HEART

PAUL FRANCIS SPENCER C.P.

As a Seal Upon Your Heart

The Life of St Paul of the Cross
Founder of the Passionists

ST PAULS

Photographs by John Pole

Graphics by Teresa Rees

ST PAULS
Middlegreen, Slough SL3 6BT, United Kingdom
Moyglare Road, Maynooth, Co. Kildare, Ireland

© ST PAULS (UK) 1994

ISBN 085439 485 0

Printed by Società San Paolo, Rome, Italy

Set me as a seal upon your heart,
as a seal upon your arm;
for love is strong as death.

Song of Songs 8:6

Contents

ABBREVIATIONS

Acta C.P.	*Acta Congregationis a SS. Cruce et Passionis D.N.J.C.*, Roma, 1930-1976
Annali	Giammaria di S. Ignazio [Cioni], *Annali della Congregazione de' Chierici Scalzi della SS.ma Croce e Passione di Gesù Cristo Nostro Signore*, Roma, 1962
Lettere	*Lettere di San Paolo della Croce*, I-IV, Roma, 1924; *ibid.*, V, Roma, 1977
Processi	*I Processi di Beatificazione e Canonizzazione di S. Paolo della Croce*, I-IV, Roma, 1969-1979
Reg. et Const.	*Regulae et Constitutiones Congr. SS.mae Crucis et Passionis D.N.J.C.* (Editio Critica Textuum), Romae, 1958
Storia	Enrico Zoffoli, *S. Paolo della Croce – Storia Critica*, I-III, Roma, 1963-1968
Storia d. Fond.	Giammaria di S. Ignazio [Cioni], *Storia delle Fondazioni*, in *Bollettino della Congregazione*, Roma, 1920-1926
Vita	Vincenzo Maria di S. Paolo [Strambi], *Vita del Ven. Servo di Dio P. Paolo della Croce, Fondatore della Congregazione de' Chierici Scalzi della SS.ma Croce, e Passione di Gesù Cristo*, Roma, 1786
Words	*Words from the Heart – A Selection from the Personal Letters of St Paul of the Cross*, ed. Mercurio and Rouse, Dublin, 1976

Preface

Saint Paul of the Cross was born on 3 January 1694. This biography has been written to commemorate the third centenary of his birth. His first biographer, St Vincent Mary Strambi, writing eleven years after his death, said that the Holy Spirit raised up Paul of the Cross to help people find God in their heart. It was Paul's lifelong conviction that God is most easily found by us in the Passion of Jesus Christ. He saw the Passion as being the most overwhelming sign of God's love and at the same time the door to union with him. His life was devoted to bringing this message to all and founding a community whose members would do the same. As a missionary, his aim was to preach the gospel as the living word of God and to do so in a language that was clear and simple. As a spiritual director and teacher of prayer, he passed on to others what he himself had learned: that when we pray, everything becomes possible. Gifted with imagination and dogged perseverance, an all too rare combination, Paul was able to see possibilities and then go on to actualise them. In his role as founder of a religious congregation he was guided by his intuitions but he also learned from his experience. Marked perhaps in his early years by a certain naivety, he was to work for fifty-five years to see the Congregation of the Passion established in the Church, carrying out his task in a spirit of fidelity to the inspiration he had been given.

No book of such modest proportions as this one could hope to do justice to this great disciple of Christ, recognised today as the most outstanding mystic of the eighteenth century. In telling the life-story of St Paul of the Cross, the text of this book highlights his mission as founder of the Passionists, while the photographs help us to enter into the world of his experience. It has been my intention to produce a book which would make St Paul of the Cross more accessible to the general public and, while hoping that the finished product is not offensive to serious scholars, I must admit that they were not uppermost in my mind.

It has been said that saints are like stained-glass windows; they let the light shine through them. As I went with John Pole to the places associated with St Paul of the Cross and watched him take the photographs used in this book, I learned a great deal about the importance of light and the different forms it has; seeing him at work was a lesson in contemplation. I am grateful to John for giving his time and his talents so generously and to Alice, his wife, for lending him to the Passionists.

My thanks are also due to the different Passionist communities we stayed with in Italy and to the members of the Passionist Secular Institute at Ovada for their kind hospitality, to Frs Diego Menoncin C.P., Antonio Curto C.P. and Michel Palud O.F.F.M. for help with transport, and to Fr Adriano Spina C.P., through whom St Paul of the Cross worked a little miracle for us. I am grateful to Patricia Goodhew for technical assistance, to Sr Miriam O'Hanrahan C.P. and James Hoyne for reading the text and giving helpful suggestions, and to the Contemplative Passionist Nuns at Daventry for giving me for several weeks a place of peace and quiet. My deepest gratitude goes to my companions Frs Marius Donnelly C.P. and Anthony Behan C.P. for their support and encouragement and for so willingly taking more than their share of parish duties to enable me to complete this labour of love.

Paul Francis Spencer C.P.
Saint Joseph's, Paris
3 January 1994

Chapter One
(1694 – 1720)

A human life is measured not just by days and months and years. For each of us there are significant moments which mark the end of one part of our life and the beginning of another. These can be encounters with persons, moves from one place to another, births, deaths, or other events which as we look back become the real measure of our lifetime more than any calendar.

For Paul Francis Danei, known to us as Saint Paul of the Cross, such a significant moment occurred when, on a day just like any other, he went to church to listen to a sermon. It probably happened in an Italian town called Campo Ligure, north of Genoa, where his family was then living. Paul, a nineteen year old student, would have been home on a visit from his college at Genoa. In the pulpit of the big parish church the priest was giving what Paul later described as a *discorso familiare*, not an elaborate sermon but a little talk in that direct and simple style which would always mean so much to him. As he sat listening to the priest, Paul was filled with such an awareness of the greatness and majesty of his Creator and of his own unworthiness of the infinite love of God that he decided there and then to give his life to God. After the sermon he went to the parish priest to make a general confession during which he was so moved by what had happened that he picked up a stone with which to beat his breast; fortunately, the priest took it from him before he could do himself any serious injury.

This experience, referred to by Paul of the Cross as his conversion to a life of penance, is the first key to understanding the meaning of the rest of his life. It was an event which shaped all that would follow, a moment which explained to him who he was before God and which gave the choices he would make in life the character of consequences. It was not that his whole life was given to him that day in a package, to be unwrapped at a later date, but what he did receive was an understanding of who God is and what claim he has, which would demand from him qualities of integrity and faithfulness as he lived out the implications of the gift of self to God he made that day.

Already at this stage we find the elements of his future way of life. He began his journey of faith after listening to a preacher. What

The Bishop of Acqui Terme celebrating Mass in the parish church at Campo Ligure

he heard gave him a sense of wonder that the all-powerful God actually loved him in a personal way. The unworthiness he felt, coupled with the overpowering truth of God's love, brought about that inner transformation which Paul called his 'conversion'. As we shall see, he had not been leading a godless life; his conversion was not the act of leaving behind a sinful past but the experience of being taken up in the hands of a loving God.

This event is the starting point of our story because it shapes what comes after it, but it too was shaped by what had gone before. Paul Francis Danei was born into a family which had its own story, and which had helped to make him the person he was as he sat that day listening to the preacher. His was an old family from the town of Castellazzo, on the road from Turin to Genoa, near Alessandria. In the Middle Ages the Danei had been involved in local government at Alessandria as notaries and officials. A good marriage into the aristocratic Trotti family, the richest people in Castellazzo, had brought them that touch of nobility with which Paul is credited by his early biographers.

His father, Luca Danei, was born on 7 December 1659, the youngest of nine children. Of the five boys in the family, only two grew to adulthood, the other being Giovanni Cristoforo, eleven years older than Luca and destined for the priesthood. At the time of Luca's birth the family was still very comfortable in economic terms, but heavy financial losses as a result of war began a process of decline which would continue during Paul's lifetime.

Some time between 1680 and 1685 Luca left Castellazzo and moved south to Ovada. There is a tradition that he went there to get married, but the truth is that he ran away to escape imprisonment, hiding in his priest-brother's house the night before he left town in order to avoid being arrested. He had been accused (wrongly, according to the family) of smuggling and was unable to return to his home town until much later, when matters had been put right with the authorities.

Eighteenth-century Italy was a collection of independent states, each with its own government and laws. By going the short distance to Ovada, Luca was leaving the Duchy of Milan and crossing the frontier into the Republic of Genoa. His father had a brother living

there, who was also a priest, and who was chaplain at the Oratory of the Confraternity of Our Lady of the Annunciation. He made his nephew welcome and helped him to find a place to stay. After a while, Luca opened a little shop, selling cloth. It was in Ovada that he met Maria Caterina De Grandis, his first wife. Her father was dead; her guardian was her uncle, Don Gaspare De Grandis, the Archpriest of Ovada. They were married on 25 February 1685 but, after five years of marriage, Maria Caterina died childless, leaving Luca a widower at the age of thirty.

The bell-towers of Ovada

After a year and a half of mourning, Luca married again. His new wife, Anna Maria Massari, was just nineteen years old. They probably met through the Confraternity of the Annunciation, of which Anna Maria had been a member since 1684. They were married in the Oratory of the Confraternity by Luca's uncle, Don Giovanni Andrea Danei, on 6 January 1692. The first of fifteen children, a girl, was born a year later on 4 January 1693 but lived only three days. She had been called Caterina, perhaps after Luca's first wife, and was the first of six children in the family to bear that name; all died in infancy except the last who lived to the age of thirty-six. Of the fifteen children Anna Maria would bear, only six survived to adulthood; all of them except Caterina lived exceptionally long lives for that time: Paul Francis was eighty-one when he died, John Baptist seventy, Teresa ninety-three, Giuseppe eighty-four and Antonio eighty-two.

Almost a year to the day after the death of little Caterina, Anna Maria held in her arms her first son, Paul Francis, born at sunrise on 3 January 1694. He was baptised three days later, his parents' second wedding anniversary. In April of the following year a second son, John Baptist, was born. Other children would follow in

Ovada. The altar in the room where St Paul of the Cross was born

The hill-top town of Cremolino

1696, 1699, 1700, 1701 and 1702, but none of them would live more than a year. This cycle of birth and death was the background to the early years of the two brothers and would be broken only with the coming of Teresa when Paul was nine years old. John Baptist, his boyhood companion, would remain close to him throughout his adult life.

During his childhood, Paul's mother was almost continually pregnant or nursing a baby. She was also in constant poor health. In spite of this, she did not neglect her two oldest sons and was always ready to share her faith with them. Paul recalled that if he cried when she was combing his hair, Anna Maria would show him a crucifix and say to him, 'See how much Jesus has suffered.' At other

19

The former Carmelite Priory at Cremolino
where Paul first went to school

times, he recalled, 'she would tell me about the lives of the saints and the austere, penitential life of the anchorites in the desert; from then on I had a great desire to serve God, and this I have always remembered.'[1] She also had a great devotion to the name of Jesus, which she communicated to her children.

Anna Maria Massari had received sufficient education to be able to read and write, skills which she passed on to her children. When Paul was seven years old, the family moved to Cremolino, about an hour's walk away, on the hillside above Ovada. Here he attended the school run by the Carmelite Fathers. The family lived more or less continuously at Cremolino for about eight years, but did not lose touch with their friends in Ovada. The parents remained as members of the Confraternity of the Annunciation which Paul also joined when he was thirteen. Anna Maria's father had been a tobacconist and Luca carried on the same business at Cremolino. Unfortunately, he got into trouble again and was imprisoned for fraud at the nearby town of Acqui Terme. While he was in prison, Monferrato, the region in which Cremolino and Acqui Terme were located, passed from the jurisdiction of the Duchy of Mantova to that of the Kingdom of Savoy. Some of Luca's friends went to the new governor to protest his innocence, claiming that he had simply taken advantage of certain privileges for tobacco trading traditionally held by Cremolino; on the basis of their testimony Luca was released. When he came out of prison, the family moved briefly to Ovada, after which they settled in Campo Ligure, a small town in the mountains, nearer to Genoa and the coast; this was probably towards the end of 1709.

Luca Danei has been described by those who knew him as good-hearted and devout, but he seems at times to have lacked the ability to manage his affairs. The moves from one place to another were always undertaken with the idea of making a fresh start in life after some period of difficulty. His lack of judgement resulted in a steady decline in the family fortune and his children, like his wife, had to learn to live with uncertainties. Of the six children who grew to adulthood, not one married.

Shortly after the family moved to Campo Ligure, Paul's youngest brother, Antonio, was born, on 4 February 1710. The house in which they lived was in the *Piazzetta della Tabaccheria*. Luca was still given to smuggling and seems to have involved his oldest sons in the business, sending them over the mountains with sacks of

The road from Campo Ligure to Genoa

tobacco. On one of these trips, Paul was shot at by brigands on his way home. He had to hand over the money he was carrying but managed to talk himself out of further danger.

Paul went to Genoa to take up his studies again. At first he found lodgings with Giuseppe Buffa, a cleric from Ovada who, although sixteen years older than him, had not yet completed his own studies. Later he stayed with the Marquis Paolo Girolamo Pallavicini. It was in Genoa that he met the mystic Maria Antonia Solimani who later founded a religious order called the Battistine, changing her name to Giovanna Battista. He often went to visit her 'to discuss spiritual matters with her or seek her advice'.[2] This was probably his first contact with the world of mystics and mysticism, with Giovanna Battista taking the role of Paul's first spiritual director. Her own spiritual director was a Capuchin, Fr Colombano da Genova, who would later direct Paul.

It was in 1713, while he was still studying at Genoa and in contact with Giovanna Battista Solimani, that Paul heard the sermon at Campo Ligure which brought about his 'conversion to a life of penance'. After this, however, he was tormented by doubts about what had happened. Had God spoken to him or was he simply deceiving himself? Was God

The old bridge at Campo Ligure

there at all, or was it all simply imagination? When these temptations against faith would come over him, he would go to church and lay his head on the altar rail because he did not know what to do. Then, on Pentecost Sunday, he was caught up in such an intense state of prayer that his doubts about the experience left him and never bothered him again. He would be faithful to his resolve to give himself completely to God, but the direction he was to take was as yet unclear.

In December 1714, the year after Paul's conversion, the Ottoman Empire declared war on Venice and the Christian West. Their immediate aim was the recovery of the Peloponnese, the southern part of Greece, which had been conquered by Venice about fifteen years earlier, after centuries of Ottoman rule. This was the site of the battle of Lepanto, the sixteenth century naval victory of Christians over Turks. Pope Clement XI tried to unite the European powers against the Ottoman forces by the Bull *Ubi primum*, published on 31 May 1715, in which he called people to fasting, almsgiving and prayer to turn away the 'anger of God', and encouraged those who could to enrol as crusading volunteers under the leadership of Venice.

Paul decided to join the crusade. John Baptist was now twenty years old and able to help their father with the business. This was Paul's chance to do something for God and perhaps even to die in defence of the faith. He went to Crema in the Republic of Venice where volunteers were being enrolled. The Venetian government was still involved in diplomatic negotiations with the other Christian states, so Paul and his fellow soldiers had to wait. Life in the army was not all that a young crusader might have expected it to be. Some of Paul's companions shared his idealistic view but others did not. After several months of marching back and forward across the plains of Lombardy, he realised that there was more involved in this war than the defence of Christendom and that army life was not for him. According to his sister Teresa, he was praying in a church in Crema during the Forty Hours Devotion when the inspiration came to him to leave the army. This was on the Thursday before Lent, 20 February 1716.[3]

Leaving Venetian territory, he went to Novello, in the diocese of

The entrance to the Church of Our Lady of Gazzo, near Sestri Ponente, with the harbour of Genoa in the background

Alba, which was in the Duchy of Milan. Here he was taken in by a married couple who had no children of their own; he lived with them for about a year. They wanted to adopt him as a son and make him their heir, but this was not what Paul had in mind. He left Novello and went to the diocese of Tortona where he stayed for about another year. What was he doing during these two years after leaving the army? As an unpaid volunteer was he free to leave the army whenever he wished, or had he deserted and gone into hiding? Was he ashamed to come home after having set out as a crusader? Or was it that he needed some time and space away from family and other pressures in order to think about his future?

During the time he was at Tortona, he kept in touch with his friends in Genoa. It was probably on his way back from one of these visits that he had another experience which helped to shape his life. In an account he wrote in 1720, he described what happened:

I was going westwards along the Riviera of Genoa when, on a hill above Sestri, I saw a small church dedicated to Our Lady of Gazzo. As soon as I saw it, my heart longed for that place of solitude, but this longing could never be satisfied – though I carried it always with me – because I was occupied by the work I was doing as a matter of charity to help my relatives. After this (I do not remember for certain either the day or the month) I remained as I was for some time but with a growing inspiration to withdraw into solitude. This inspiration, accompanied by great tenderness of heart, was given me by the good God.[4]

Meanwhile Paul's uncle, the priest Don Cristoforo, perhaps thinking that there was no point in leaving the family property to Luca, had decided to make Paul his heir. He invited him to move to his house in Castellazzo, which Paul did in 1718. Freed from his involvement in his father's business and supported by his uncle, Paul was able to live as he pleased. He dedicated himself to a life of prayer, following the inspiration he had received, while waiting for the opportunity to 'withdraw into solitude'. His uncle thought that his heir should marry and settle down, so he found him a suitable wife, but Paul informed him that he could not marry her as he had taken a vow of chastity. Don Cristoforo wrote to Rome for a dispensation, then continued the arrangements for the marriage. There was nothing Paul could do except leave the future in God's hands; he prayed that some obstacle would arise so that he would be able to follow his inspiration.

In the end the two families could not agree on the girl's dowry and the marriage negotiations broke down. Shortly afterwards, on 16 November 1718, Don Cristoforo died. He had left all the family property and money to Paul on condition that he would marry; the inheritance was valued at twelve thousand *scudi*, the equivalent of about three thousand pounds sterling at that time, which was a considerable sum. When the will was read, in the sacristy of the church of San Carlo in Castellazzo, Paul renounced the inheritance

The Oratory of the Confraternity of St Anthony of the Desert, Castellazzo

in favour of his brothers and sisters, saying that he wished to keep for himself only a breviary. According to St Vincent Mary Strambi, his first biographer, he turned to the crucifix in the sacristy and said, 'My crucified Lord, I protest that I want none of this inheritance except this breviary, since you alone are enough for me, my God, my only Good.'[5]

Around the time of his uncle's death, Paul's parents and brothers and sisters moved to Castellazzo. His father was now sixty years old and seems to have given up business, devoting himself to the care of the family property. The population of Castellazzo was about four thousand. As well as a number of oratories and a monastery of Augustinian nuns, there were four main churches in the town. These were the Capuchin church, the Augustinian church of San Martino, where the members of the Danei family were buried, the parish church of San Carlo e Sant'Anna in the care of the diocesan clergy and Paul's own parish church, Santa Maria, which belonged to the Servites.

According to Fr Giammaria Cioni, who was his confessor for the last ten years of his life, Paul described his life at Castellazzo during this period as follows:

Between daytime and night I used to spend at least seven hours in prayer and other religious activities. On feast day mornings I used to rise very early to attend a confraternity of which I was a member. After the confraternity, I would go to the main church where, as was customary, the Blessed Sacrament was exposed, and would remain there at least five hours on my knees. After that I would go for something to eat, and then I would go to Vespers. After Vespers, I would take a little fresh air with some devout young men and talk with them about spiritual things. Last, I would visit the church of the Capuchins where I would spend an hour in mental prayer; then I would return home.[6]

Paul had joined the Confraternity of St Anthony of the Desert, which met in the oratory down the street from his home; after a short time he was elected prior. The members of the confraternity would meet on Sundays and feast days to listen to him read from some book on prayer, which he would then try to explain to them.

Crucifix in the church of San Martino, Castellazzo

*Santa Maria in Castellazzo,
parish church of the Danei family*

It was probably at this time that he discovered the *Treatise on the Love of God* of St Francis de Sales, which gave him an understanding of the life of prayer which he was able to pass on to others.

While living with his family at Castellazzo, Paul was noted for his kindness to the poor. His sister Teresa found him on his knees one day offering food to a poor woman. His mother had to warn him not to give everything away; she said she was afraid he would come home naked some day. He began practising abstinence, training himself for his penitential life. He gave up eating the muscatel grapes which grew in the garden, although he was very fond of them. On Fridays he would drink a mixture of gall and vinegar in remembrance of the Passion of Jesus. He kept it discreetly in a flask, but Teresa broke it one day by accident while she was trying to find out what was in it. As soon as she discovered his secret, she ran off to tell an aunt of theirs who was an Augustinian nun.

With John Baptist as his companion, Paul would rise two or three hours before dawn to pray in the attic. On one occasion, their father caught them scourging themselves with a discipline of leather thongs, a common penitential practice in those days. He snatched it from them, shouting at them, 'Do you want to kill yourselves?'[7]

As time passed after the experience of Sestri, Paul had felt God's call taking a more definite form. He wrote:

I had the idea of wearing a poor black tunic of coarse cloth called arbagio, the ordinary wool fabric found in these parts, of going barefoot, of living in very deep poverty – in short, by God's grace, leading a penitential life. This never again left my heart. I had an even greater inclination not simply to retire to the little chapel mentioned above; it would be enough for me to withdraw into solitude either there or anywhere else. This I would do in response to God's loving invitation, for in his infinite goodness he was calling me to leave the world.[8]

At one stage Paul became ill with fever. In a state of delirium, he began shouting blasphemies against God, the Virgin Mary and, strange to say, the town of Ovada. His family had to send for a doctor to give him a sedative. When he was recovering, two Capuchins came from the friary to visit him. While they were in his room, the ever-curious Teresa listened at the door. She heard him say to the priests 'Oh, how long eternity is!', from which she concluded that he must have had a vision of hell; but when she asked Paul, he refused to tell her what had happened.

Paul was tall, dark and handsome, and on more than one occasion he found himself the object of the attentions of the young ladies of Castellazzo. The girl his uncle had wanted him to marry was infatuated with him and would follow him around, as did some of the other girls in the town. One of them even tried making a proposition to him while he was praying in church. However, Paul had a different aim in life. In order to discourage his admirers, he stopped looking after his appearance: he would not shave or cut his fingernails and did not bother to change his clothes. He would be seen in the streets of the town with his eyes cast down and his arms crossed over his breast, going to or from one of the churches. But, in spite of his strange appearance, he was no morbid eccentric. He had a large circle of friends who shared his interests and were always happy to be with him. He would give them the benefits of his study and spiritual experience. Many of these young men later

The old church and friary of the Capuchins, Castellazzo

29

became priests or religious. One of them, Francesco Antonio Capriata, who later became a Capuchin, recalled receiving instructions from Paul 'on mental prayer, regarding the purgative, illuminative and unitive ways, in which I remember he used a great deal, as he did in everything, the doctrine of St Francis de Sales, of which he had a wonderful grasp.'[9]

In the midst of all this, he was still sure that God was calling him to something more. He had, he tells us, 'another inspiration to gather companions who would live together in unity and promote the fear of God in souls.'[10] The crusading spirit was not dead in him; he knew that to be a disciple meant taking up the Cross. One day as he prayed, he felt the words 'I will show you how much you must suffer for the sake of my name'[11] echoing within his innermost self. As he poured out his heart in the presence of the Blessed Sacrament, he received the words: 'Son, he who embraces me embraces thorns.'[12] An image which came to him in prayer several times he describes as follows:

When I was at prayer I saw a scourge in God's hands, and this scourge had lashes like a discipline and on them was written the word: LOVE. In that very moment God gave me a profound understanding that he wished to scourge me but with love. My soul ran quickly to embrace the scourge and to kiss it in spirit. Actually when God in his infinite goodness had let me see this, special troubles befell me shortly afterwards, and I knew for certain that they were coming because God had given me an infused understanding of them.[13]

It was at Castellazzo that Paul received the Sacrament of Confirmation from the Bishop of Alessandria on 23 April 1719. He was twenty-five years old, which was not an unusual age for confirmation at that time; the bishop only came to Castellazzo for confirmation every ten years. The ceremony took place in the Servite parish church of Santa Maria, near Paul's home.

Paul had learned from Giovanna Battista Solimani the importance of spiritual direction. Feeling the need for guidance, he went to the parish priest, who was a rigid, austere man and a hypochondriac. His way of forming Paul was to humiliate him. He would keep him waiting for hours at the confessional and pass him by when giving out Holy Communion. On feast days, when there were crowds of people at Mass, he would order him to kneel out in the middle of the church. Paul did it out of obedience, but used to go scarlet with embarrassment. On one occasion he put flowers behind Paul's ears and wanted him to wear them going about the town. Eventually, he admitted to being out of his depth and suggested that he should go to someone else for guidance.

Paul turned to the Guardian of the Capuchin Friary, Fr Girolamo da Tortona. Fr Girolamo advised him to receive Communion every day, but suggested that he should do so in different churches, so as not to draw attention to himself, as frequent Communion was uncommon at the time. He was more understanding and supportive and, when he felt he had given as much as he could, he passed Paul on to his fellow Capuchin Fr Colombano da Genova, Giovanna Battista Solimani's director.

It was while he was being directed by the Capuchins that Paul received an indication of what he was to become. Writing towards the end of 1720 he says:

This last summer (I do not remember the day or the month because I did not write it down but I do know it was the grain harvest time) on a certain weekday in the Capuchin church in Castellazzo, I received holy Communion with a deep sense of my unworthiness. I remember that I was deeply recollected and then I left to go home. Walking along the street I was as recollected as if I were at prayer. When I came to a street corner to turn towards home, I was raised up in God in the deepest recollection, with complete forgetfulness of all else and with great interior peace. At that moment I saw myself clothed in a long black garment with a white cross on my breast, and below the cross the holy name of Jesus was written in white letters. At that instant I heard these very words spoken to me: 'This signifies how pure and spotless that heart should be which must bear the holy name of Jesus graven upon it.' On seeing and hearing this I began to weep and then it stopped.

Shortly afterwards I saw in spirit the tunic presented to me with the holy name of Jesus and the cross all in white, but the tunic was black. I pressed it joyfully to my heart.[14]

This idea of wearing a black garment with the name of Jesus and a white cross on the front of it was linked with the other inspirations to withdraw into solitude, to live a penitential life and to gather companions to promote reverence for God. Together they provided the basic structure for a way of responding to the love of God Paul had experienced at the moment of his conversion. In the text quoted above Paul goes on to say:

After these visions of the tunic and the sign, God gave me a stronger compelling desire to gather companions and with the approval of holy Mother Church to found a Congregation called: 'The Poor of Jesus'. After this God infused in my soul in a lasting manner the form of the holy Rule to be observed by the Poor of Jesus and by me his least and lowest servant… Let it be known that the intention God gave me with regard to this Congregation was none other than this: in the first place, to observe God's law perfectly together with the perfect observance of his evangelical counsels, especially by total detachment from all created things with the perfect practice of holy poverty, so essential for the observance of the other counsels and for maintaining fervour at prayer; in the second place to have zeal for God's glory, to promote the fear of God in souls by working for the destruction of sin, in a word, to be indefatigable in works of charity that our beloved God may be loved, feared, served and praised by all for ever and ever. Amen.[15]

Paul explained to Fr Columbano that he believed that God was calling him to 'found a Congregation called the Poor of Jesus'. The Capuchin gave his approval but could do no more than encourage the idea. If Paul were to take steps to bring this about, he would need the consent of the bishop. As a first step he went to Alessandria and told his story to Don Paolo Policarpo Cerruti, the Canon Penitentiary of the Cathedral. Canon Cerruti was suspicious of all this mysticism and told Paul to forget about it and meditate instead on sin, death and the judgement of God. For a time he tried Paul's sincerity with tactics not unlike those of the parish priest at Castellazzo. In the end he was convinced of the authenticity of Paul's inspirations and said that he should see the bishop.

The Bishop of Alessandria was Monsignor Francesco Maria

*Bishop Francesco
Maria Arboreo di Gattinara*

Arboreo di Gattinara. Born on 13 January 1658, he was about two years older than Paul's father. A former Provincial Superior of the Congregation of the Clerics Regular of St Paul, commonly known as the Barnabites, he had been Bishop of Alessandria for fourteen years. He received Paul at his palace and asked him to explain what was on his mind. Paul began by making a general confession, then shared with the bishop the inspirations he had received about wearing the black tunic, going barefoot, living in poverty. As he told his story, the bishop was moved to tears. When he had finished, Monsignor Gattinara suggested that he should write it all down. He also thought that Paul should seek advice from the most learned and devout men in the region, and later arranged for him to meet two Jesuits whose opinion he respected.

After a period of discernment, Bishop Gattinara agreed to clothe Paul in the black tunic and let him begin his 'penitential life'. Paul got hold of some of the rough wool cloth called *arbagio* worn by poor people in the country around Genoa. According to Teresa, it was the bishop who paid for it. After Paul had had the cloth dyed black so as to look like what he had seen in the vision, Teresa herself made the tunic. It was like a large sack with sleeves, gathered at the waist by

The courtyard of the Bishop's Palace, Alessandria

a belt made from the same cloth. The coarse wool would be uncomfortable next to his skin. The sign he had seen in the vision, the white cross with the name of Jesus under it, he would not be able to wear until many years later. Instead, he would wear a crucifix on his breast.

The date set for Paul to receive the tunic was 22 November. He had thought of the twenty-first, feast of the Presentation of Mary in the Temple, a feast which spoke to him about giving oneself to God, but as the following day was a Friday, he decided to wait until then in honour of the Passion of Christ. As the day approached, Paul began to have second thoughts. Years later he wrote:

> I experienced interior desolation, depression, doubts. It seemed to me that I would never be able to persevere in my vocation. The devil suggested to me that I was deceived, that I could serve God in some other way, that this was no kind of life for me, etc., and other such things that I pass over in silence. To crown my misfortune, all devotion had vanished. I felt dry and was tried in every way. Even the sound of the church bells disturbed me. Everyone seemed happy except me! I can never hope to explain these fierce assaults, and I was more strongly attacked by them when I was about to be vested in the habit and to leave my poor home.[16]

In spite of these difficulties, he decided to go ahead, believing that this was what God wanted him to do. On 21 November he had his hair cut short, as a sign of his changed way of life. That night, he sat at supper thinking of what lay ahead, as did the other members of the family; he would be leaving early next morning, so this was the time for farewells. It was not that he would never see his family again, but that he would not belong to them nor they to him in the way it had been until now. He was leaving home to begin a new way of life. After the meal the family knelt, as usual, to say the rosary. When it was finished, Paul remained on his knees to ask a blessing from his father and mother. Then he prayed the *Te Deum* in thanksgiving for all he had received through his family and Psalm 50, the *Miserere*, to signify that he was now going to live as a penitent.

The following day he set out early to walk to Alessandria, with the tunic in a parcel under his arm. He later said that as he walked to the bishop's palace on that late November morning, he was full of fear and apprehension: he wondered if he would be able to go barefoot or if the cold would prove too much for him. When he arrived at the residence, he was told that the bishop had gone to nearby Bosco Marengo (later to be made famous by Napoleon) and that he would not be back that day. Paul asked if he could wait; he was sure the bishop would return. Monsignor Gattinara did indeed arrive that evening and brought Paul upstairs to his private chapel where the simple ceremony of blessing and imposition of the black tunic of a penitent took place.

For the bishop, what happened that evening was the clothing ceremony of a hermit; he was prepared to allow Paul to set out on this new way of life and watch what would happen. Hermits were not uncommon in eighteenth-century Italy, living alone, caring for remote chapels and oratories. This one wanted to teach catechism and help people to pray, and that was not a bad thing. As we shall see later, he was not so sure about the idea of founding a new religious order, but was willing to give Paul a chance. For Paul, and for those who would come after him, that ceremony in the bishop's chapel had another meaning: it was the beginning of the Poor of Jesus, later to be known as the Congregation of the Passion.

According to one of his friends, Paulo Sardi, Paul stayed that night in Alessandria. It had been arranged by himself and the bishop that he would go to the church of San Carlo to make a retreat of forty days, during which he would write an account of the different inspirations he had received. He would also keep a diary of what happened during the retreat and would put on paper the rule of life for his congregation of the Poor of Jesus.

Paul went back to Castellazzo the next morning, arriving early enough to be at Mass. He did not return to his own home but went after Mass to the little room behind the sacristy which, though damp and rough-and-ready, was to be his hermitage for the next forty days. He caused some excitement when he was seen at Mass barefoot and clothed in the black tunic. Paulo Sardi and some of his other friends heard he was there and ran to the church to see him and to find out what had happened the day before; then they went home and left him there, alone with God.

NOTES

1. *Processi*, I, 311.
2. Musso, G., *Una mistica del secolo XVIII*, Genova, 1960 (quoted in Bialas, Martin, *The Mysticism of the Passion in St Paul of the Cross*, San Francisco, Ignatius Press, 1990, p. 127.
3. *Processi*, II, 25.
4. *Words*, 11.
5. *Vita*, 17.
6. *Processi*, I, 32.
7. *Ibid.*, II, 29.
8. *Words*, 11.
9. *Processi*, II, 50.
10. *Words*, 12.
11. cf. Acts 9: 16.
12. *Processi*, I, 126.
13. *Words*, 13.
14. *Ibid.*, 12.
15. *Ibid.*, 13f.
16. *Ibid.*, 143.

Chapter Two
(1720 – 1721)

'Thanks be to God and to the ever-virgin Mary.'[1] With these words Paul began the day-by-day recording of his inspirations and temptations, the desolations and consolations of his desert experience. As a result of Bishop Gattinara's request that he keep a written account of his prayer and inner states, there has come down to us a spiritual diary which, though covering only a forty day period, is a classic text of Catholic mysticism.

The retreat was for him a time of entering deeply into that interior desert in which he would imitate Jesus himself, seeking to be faithful to prayer, struggling with the forces of evil, and allowing his heart to be purified so that he might be intent only on seeking God's will. It was also the time for him to write the rule of life for the Poor of Jesus. However, Paul was well aware that the writing of the Rule would only be possible for him if he were attentive to the voice of the Spirit speaking in the depths of his heart. Realising that the wisdom which must guide him was not merely human wisdom, he placed himself at the foot of the Cross, writing on the first day of his retreat, 23 November 1720: 'God makes me understand that …temptations purify the soul. I know that, by the mercy of our dear God, I desire to know nothing else nor to taste any consolation; my sole desire is to be crucified with Jesus.'[2]

From the diary we see that his relationship with God was founded on the felt awareness of the reality of God's love as shown in the Passion. He writes on 26 November:

I know that I also held colloquies on the sorrowful Passion of my beloved Jesus. When I speak to him of his sufferings, for example, I say: 'Ah, my Supreme Good! What were the sentiments of your Sacred Heart when you were scourged? My beloved Spouse, how greatly did the sight of my grievous sins and my ingratitude afflict you! Ah, my only Love, why do I not die for you? Why am I not overwhelmed with sorrow?' And then I feel that sometimes my spirit can say no more but remains thus in God with his sufferings infused into the soul – and sometimes it seems as if my heart would break.[3]

The church of San Carlo at Castellazzo

39

At first sight, this kind of language seems far removed from our present-day ways of talking about prayer. Yet even across the cultural barriers which separate us from the eighteenth century, we sense the extraordinary closeness to Jesus in his suffering experienced by Paul, and recognise that it was love which brought this about. Nor was it a merely sentimental love, divorced from the realities of life. Alongside such experiences Paul had to contend with the uncertainties involved in embarking on a new way of life as he prepared to write a Rule for a community of which he was, as yet, the only member. The same day he wrote:

For the rest of the day, especially in the evening, I was greatly troubled and depressed... and although this depression does not take away peace of heart, there is a great dread that neither spiritual consolations nor anything else will ever come again – and it seems as if they were never present before either. I know that I told my Jesus that his crosses are the joys of my heart.[4]

In spite of these inner struggles, he held on to his conviction that what he was involved in was no less than a work of God and that his real consolation lay in being faithful to the inspiration he had received. Already, in the first days of the retreat, he wanted to go to Rome, as did Francis of Assisi, Ignatius Loyola and others, to ask the pope to bless and confirm what he believed God was calling him to do. On 27 November, he wrote:

I know that I had a particular urge to go to Rome for this great and wonderful work of God. I also asked my Sovereign Good if it were his will that I should write the Rule for the Poor of Jesus, and I felt a strong urge to do so, with great sweetness. I rejoiced that our great God should wish to make use of so great a sinner, and on the other hand, I knew not where to cast myself, knowing myself to be so wretched. Enough! I know that I tell my beloved Jesus that all creatures shall sing his mercies.[5]

Five days later, he started writing the Rule for the Poor of Jesus, in which the form of life which had been clarified during the different founding experiences was to be expressed. He wrote in the sacristy, where there was a desk and all the necessary materials:

Paul writing the Rule for the Poor of Jesus

I began to write this Rule in the year 1720 on 2 December and finished on the 7th of the same month. Before writing I said Matins before daybreak and spent some time in mental prayer. Then I left prayer full of courage and began to write. The infernal enemy did not fail to assault me by stirring up feelings of repugnance within me and making difficulties about my doing this. But since God had inspired me to this task and as I had been given orders to do it, without more ado by God's grace I set to work.

Let it be known that when I was writing, I wrote as quickly as if some one were dictating to me; I felt the words coming from the heart. I have written this to make it known that this was a special inspiration from God because as for myself I am but wickedness and ignorance.

In all, however, I submit to the judgement of my superiors. May the Blessed Sacrament on all the altars of the whole world be praised and adored by all.[6]

The Sacrament of the Eucharist strengthened him for the work of writing the Rule, and many of the inspirations he received during

The room at San Carlo where Paul
made his retreat of forty days

the retreat were associated with the Eucharist (as had been the case with the first vision of the habit). He wrote on 4 December:

At holy Communion I had much sweetness. My dear God gave me infused knowledge of the joy which the soul will have when we see him face to face, when it will be united with him in holy love. Then I felt sorrow to see him offended and I told him that I would willingly be torn to pieces for a single soul. Indeed, I felt that I would die when I saw the loss of so many souls who do not experience the fruit of the Passion of Jesus.[7]

Reaching out to those who were not experiencing the love of God, fruit of the Passion of Jesus, would be the mission of the Poor of Jesus. Paul believed that God wanted this new community to be founded so that his love could touch the hearts of those who felt cut off from him. On 7 December, the day on which he finished the text of the Rule, Paul wrote:

I had likewise great fervour mingled with tears in praying for the conversion of poor sinners; I kept telling God that I could no longer bear to see him offended. I had also special tenderness in imploring God in his mercy to found the holy Congregation quickly, and to send forth some people for his greater glory and for the good of their neighbours – this with great desire and fervour. I asked him to accept me as the least and lowest servant of his poor, and it seemed to me that I was utterly unworthy (as indeed I am) to serve him as a scullion.[8]

The Passion of Jesus moved Paul to want to reach out to others because its message had already penetrated his own heart. The remembrance of the Passion was for him a privileged place of encounter with God. In the text of the diary for 8 December, he gave this description of his way of praying:

At holy Communion I was particularly recollected, especially in a sorrowful and loving remembrance of the sufferings of my Jesus.
This high favour which the good God grants me at such a time I

*know not how to explain because I cannot. You must know that, in
recalling the sufferings of my dear Jesus, sometimes when I have only
recalled one or two I have to stop because the soul can say no more
and feels that it is melting away. It remains thus languishing with the
greatest sweetness mingled with tears, with the sufferings of the Spouse
infused into it; or to explain it more clearly, it is immersed in the
Heart and in the sorrows of its beloved Spouse, Jesus. Sometimes it
understands them all, and remains thus in God in this loving and
sorrowful contemplation.*

*It is very difficult to explain; it always seems to me to be some-
thing new.*[9]

This loving and sorrowful contemplation was the core of his
spirituality and the means by which the Congregation was to
accomplish its mission. In the Rule for the Poor of Jesus he had
written:

*Dearly beloved, you must know that the main object in wearing
black (according to the special inspiration that God gave me) is to be
clothed in mourning for the Passion and Death of Jesus. For this
purpose let us never forget to have always with us a constant and
sorrowful remembrance of him. And so let each of the Poor of Jesus
take care to instil in others meditation on the suffering of our Jesus.*[10]

For Paul, the retreat was a time of entering deeply into the
mystery of the sufferings of Jesus; it was also an experience of the
meaning of the mystery of his own suffering, in which he learned
how God could purify his heart through his own inner struggles.
He wrote on 21 December:

*I would like to make everyone understand the great grace that God,
in his mercy, bestows when he sends suffering, especially suffering de-
void of consolation. Then indeed the soul is purified like gold in the
furnace; without knowing it, it becomes radiant and is set free to take
flight to its Good, that is to the blessed transformation. It carries the
cross with Jesus and knows it not... I understand that this is a great
and fruitful way of suffering, most pleasing to God, because the soul*

thereby becomes indifferent to such an extent that it no longer thinks of sorrow or joy but solely of remaining conformed to the holy will of its beloved Spouse, Jesus.[11]

During the last days of the retreat, Paul's love of the Eucharist moved him to pray for England. On the feast of St Stephen, 26 December, he prayed for the people of 'England and the neighbouring kingdoms'. This prayer was linked with a desire 'to die a martyr's death in a place where the adorable mystery of the Eucharist is denied.'[12] Three days later, on the feast of St Thomas of Canterbury, he wrote:

I had a particular impulse to pray for the conversion of England, especially because I want the standard of the holy Faith to be erected so that there will be an increase of devotion and reverence, of homage and love, with frequent acts of adoration for the Blessed Sacrament, the ineffable mystery of God's most holy love, and so that his holy Name may be glorified in a very special way. The desire to die as a martyr, especially for the Blessed Sacrament, in some place where people do not believe, does not leave me.[13]

Why should someone living in a small town in the north of Italy have had this interest in 'England and the neighbouring kingdoms'? From his reading of St Francis de Sales, he would have been familiar with St Thomas of Canterbury as one who died 'by and for divine love'.[14] Castellazzo, Ovada and Campo Ligure were all on the route taken by those going to Rome from England and returning to England from Rome. Was it the memory of the priests of the *Venerabile* (the English College in Rome), those 'future martyrs' revered by St Philip Neri which gave him this desire to pray and work for the healing of divisions between Christians in 'England and the neighbouring kingdoms'?

Paul concluded his forty day retreat on Wednesday, 1 January 1721. It had been a test of endurance not just on account of the cold weather and the confinement, but also because of the experiences of desolation he had to undergo, even on Christmas Day, when he had written: 'At holy Communion I was as dry as a stump and I remained so nearly all day.' On this last day of the retreat at least, he was consoled at the reception of the Eucharist; he wrote:

Through the infinite love of our dear God I was raised up in spirit to great recollection and many tears especially after holy Communion during which I felt keenly the sweetness of holy love. It seemed to me that I was melting away in God.

...When serving mass, I had such a deep light on the great love which God displays towards me, and on my misery, my ingratitude, my whole life, that I did not venture even to raise my eyes to look upon the picture of Mary – and always with abundance of tears mingled with great sweetness especially on seeing my Spouse, Jesus, present in the Blessed Sacrament.[15]

His retreat over and the texts of the Rule and his diary in his hand, Paul set out for Alessandria to find out from the bishop what he should do next. As he entered the bishop's palace, what thoughts or expectations was he also carrying with him? The last time they had met was on 22 November, the day Paul had been clothed in the black tunic. Now, six weeks later, on 2 January, he came back to present Monsignor Gattinara with the 'Rule to be observed by the Poor of Jesus'. Paul knew that there were other young men who with a little encouragement would become part of this new community: for example, his brother John Baptist and his good friend Paolo Sardi. In fact, Fr Columbano had already written to the bishop on 26 November recommending to him Antonio Schiaffino and Michelangelo Michelini, two of Paul's other companions, who wanted to receive the tunic and 'take on the austere life of the Institute, ...withdrawing [into solitude] with Paul'.[16] The next step was to go to Rome and receive the pope's approval so that together with the others he could live the gospel vision contained in the Rule of the Poor of Jesus.

The bishop read the text carefully: it was composed of about twenty little chapters, obviously written by a very sincere young man, who was full of the Spirit but who had, on his own admission, never read the Rule of an established religious order and who certainly knew nothing about the ways of the Roman Curia. Coming as he did from an old noble family which had been dealing with popes for centuries, Bishop Gattinara had no illusions about Paul's chances of having his Rule approved by the pope. He advised him that this was not the time to be thinking of a trip to Rome. A better idea would be to visit Fr Columbano in order to let him read the new Rule.

Paul set off for Pontedecimo, just north of Genoa, where Fr Columbano was living. As he travelled barefoot over the snow-covered hills, clothed in the rough black tunic, the realities of his new way of life were brought home to him. The bishop thought that the hardships of the journey would strengthen his resolve to do God's will. The treacherous condition of the roads would have made the sixty or so kilometres from Alessandria to Pontedecimo seem much longer. On the night of 6 January, Paul reached the Boccheta Pass, after which it was downhill towards the coast. The next morning, as he was standing in the sun, trying to warm himself, a group of policemen passed by. One of them, feeling sorry for him, came back, excused himself, and handed him some bread, apologising for not having anything else to give. As he came nearer to Genoa, he met other people on the road, some of whom had some fun at his expense, saying that he must be either a saint or a great sinner to be wandering the roads dressed so miserably and carrying only a breviary.

Fr Columbano read the text and pronounced it to be 'a true holy Rule, fit to be submitted for approval to the Holy See';[17] the simplicity of the friar seemed to be at variance with the wisdom of the prelate. Paul returned to Alessandria, encouraged by the holy Capuchin, to be told by Bishop Gattinara that he would have to wait for a while. Was it on this occasion that Paul, always convinced of what he was called to do, was asked by the bishop, 'How is that you get all the inspirations? I could do with a few inspirations myself!'[18]

Looking back at the relationship between Paul and the bishop, we cannot help admiring the openness of Gattinara, that a man in his position and with his experience would take seriously the 'vision' of a twenty-six year old layman. He sent Paul to live at the hermitage attached to the church of Trinità da lungi, about two miles from Castellazzo and told him that he could begin forming groups for catechesis at the parish church of San Carlo.

Set in open country, Trinità da lungi had in the Middle Ages belonged to the Cistercians. Nothing remained now of the former priory and hospice except the Romanesque church and the little hermitage built alongside it. It was the nearest thing in the Castellazzo area to a 'place of solitude' such as Paul desired, and indeed it was perhaps at his own suggestion that he was sent there by the bishop. However, because it was distant from the town, the Blessed Sacrament was not reserved in the church and Mass was rarely celebrated there. Paul quickly realised that from this important point of view it was really unsuitable. Consequently, after staying there just a couple of weeks, he moved on Saturday 25 January to the hermitage of Santo Stefano, on the edge of the town and just five minutes walk from the church of the Capuchins.

Two days later, he wrote to the bishop to tell him that he had begun his catechetical work and that he was sending Paolo Sardi to see him. 'As is my duty,' he wrote, 'I did not wish to be remiss in informing Your Excellency of what I frequently receive from God about this earnest servant of his. You must know, Bishop, that I am inspired to think that he will be my companion in wearing this same holy habit.'[19] The bishop's reaction is not recorded; we do know that Sardi never received the habit and ended his days as a Canon at Alessandria. In the same letter, Paul thanked the bishop for sending him to Santo Stefano, 'a solitude that is a real paradise', and described to him his first experience of his new ministry:

On Sunday, that is yesterday, I began to go around with the bell and cross inviting people to praise God and attend Christian Doctrine. By God's mercy everything went well in an orderly way. For the first time quite a number of people turned up and I was very fervent in speaking the Word of God... I must not omit to tell you that the devil used all his infamous arts (I do not list them here, to avoid undue length) to interrupt this work of God. It is enough for me to say: 'I can do all things in him who strengthens me.' I now clearly see that this is God's holy Will.[20]

In his letter to the bishop, Paul did not mention the other feelings which accompanied his first efforts as a catechist. Years later, he told one of his companions that when he went out for the first time to invite the people to come to his instructions at the parish church of San Carlo, he was blushing with embarrassment as he did so. However, in spite of his embarrassment, the classes were a great success and, on the strength of the good report sent by the parish priest, the bishop authorised Paul to preach from the pulpit in San Carlo every Sunday. His method in preaching was to choose one or two verses of Scripture which appealed to him and talk to the people about them. So grateful were the people for his words that after the sermon, crowds would follow him to Santo Stefano and ask him to preach to them again. His brother Antonio, who was eleven years old at the time, recalled one such occasion: 'I remember seeing and hearing him preach in Santo Stefano; he was speaking about the Passion of Jesus Christ with extraordinary fervour, not, however, from the pulpit in San Carlo but from the balustrade in Santo Stefano, which had some steps leading up to it.'[21]

The church and hermitage of
Trinità da Lungi, outside Castellazzo

The crypt of the church of
Santo Stefano

The hermitage at Santo Stefano became a meeting place for the group of young men who had gathered around Paul. Here they would come to pray with him, and to share a meal made from the food placed by passers-by in a basket Paul had left outside the church. He had put a sign beside it which read: 'Give alms for the poor of Jesus Christ'. The best of what was put there he gave to the poor, who came in large numbers to be fed by him, while he generally took what was left over to feed himself and any of his friends who wanted to share his meal. Occasionally he would give everything away and have nothing left to eat, as his father discovered one day when he visited him at the hermitage. He told Paul that he would go home and have some food sent to him but, according to Teresa, Paul thanked him for the offer but refused to accept. Luca replied that he would have to accept it as an act of obedience and, no doubt smiling at having caught Paul by means of his own virtue, he went home and had Teresa prepare a pot of soup.[22] Paul's brother John Baptist came there often to eat with him, as did his good friend Paulo Sardi, who would say the Divine Office with him before sitting down to a meal of bread and water. The water came from the nearby well which Paul used to refer to as his 'wine cellar'. Like John Baptist, Paulo Sardi hoped to be able to join Paul in his new way of life. One day while it was still winter, he decided to try going barefoot but, after going about forty steps, he could take no more and had to go home for his shoes.

As Lent drew near, Paul's attention focused on the carnival, a time of relaxation before the Lenten fast which had degenerated into an excuse for excesses in drinking, dancing and immoral behaviour. The cloistered Augustinian nuns of Castellazzo used to admit people in fancy dress into the parlour during the carnival. Often these revellers would be in no condition to be seen anywhere, least of all in a monastery. Paul had advised his aunt, who was a member of the community, that such goings-on were not appropriate for those seeking to live a contemplative life, but his advice was not taken seriously. One evening, as he was passing the monastery, he saw a group wearing carnival masks going inside. With his crucifix in hand, he ran in after them and gave both revellers and nuns an impromptu sermon which was effective in ending the practice.

As the carnival progressed, so did Paul's attempt to prepare the townspeople for Lent. None of the usual excesses were to be seen in Castellazzo that year. On the evening of the last Sunday of the carnival, the streets of the town were deserted; all the people had gone to San Carlo to hear Paul preach. He appeared in the pulpit wearing a crown of thorns, with a rope around his neck. He preached for about two hours. Years later he would say that this sermon had borne more fruit than a dozen missions.[23]

Not everyone was impressed by his work. One of the Capuchins, perhaps a little jealous, said: 'What could someone who hasn't studied have to say? Apart from doing a bit of meditation on Gethsemane and on the Passion, he doesn't know anything else.' However, the witness who remembered these words was himself converted by Paul's preaching.[24]

During Lent, he preached every day at Santo Stefano, in the morning or afternoon to the women and in the evening to the men. His work consisted in teaching the people how to approach the Sacrament of Reconciliation, promoting among them love and reverence for Jesus in the Eucharist, instructing them about the

Christian Faith and showing them how to meditate on the Passion of Christ. After the Passion meditation, he would finish with a hymn about the Passion, the words of which he wrote himself. In preparing people for confession, Paul not only gave instruction to large groups, but also helped individuals who were afraid of going to a priest or who did not know how to confess their sins. Not being a priest himself, he was unable to absolve the people of their sins, so he would write a note for them to bring to one of those confessors in Castellazzo or Alessandria whom he knew were more experienced and willing to help those in difficulty. One day he met one of these priests who joked with him saying, 'What do you think you are up to? We confessors aren't even getting time to eat!'[25]

Like the confessors, Paul himself seems to have had plenty to do. There were at least thirty secular priests and three communities of sisters among his supporters. Some of the priests would come to Santo Stefano to consult him; a number of them took up the practice of meditation, instructed by Paul. During Lent he was also invited by the Augustinian nuns to come and preach to them. He wrote to Bishop Gattinara:

My dear Bishop and Father in the Lord,

The nuns of this locality wish to hear the word of God from the mouth of this big sinner. Reverend Mother has informed me through her agent. I am anxious to help these good religious by encouraging them to ever greater perfection. Therefore (as is my duty) I now request Your Excellency's permission freely to proclaim religious perfection to these good religious. I beg you to grant me this permission with your blessing. The conferences (with your permission) will be on Monday, Thursday and Saturday, accompanied in each case with a devout meditation.[26]

In the midst of all this activity Paul had not forgotten that God had called him to 'gather companions' to help him in his ministry and to live with him in a praying community. He told the bishop in the same letter that he felt an 'ever stronger inspiration to leave for

*Crucifix in the church of
Santo Stefano, Castellazzo*

Rome'. Before doing this, he wanted to make a pilgrimage to the shrine at Monte Varallo, a centre of devotion to the Passion. On returning to Castellazzo he would, he said, continue to teach Christian Doctrine to the people, inviting them to persevere and warning them of the dangers of falling away; 'then, with your blessing,' he continued, 'I will leave to go to the feet of His Holiness – this is my great wish.' He then pleads with the bishop to allow him to do this, explaining to him how important it is:

Reverend and dear Pastor, for the love of Jesus Christ I beg you to be kind enough to grant me this permission so that I may follow the inspirations of my Spouse, Jesus Christ. I will say nothing about companions as I know for sure that when I am at the feet of His Holiness, God will make the whole world see his mercies. So much do I trust in my crucified Lord that I am more than certain everything will turn out well. God has given me the inspiration and an absolutely certain sign of what he wills. Why should I fear? Were I to doubt this, it seems to me that I would commit a sin of infidelity.[27]

After signing the letter 'Your most humble son and servant, Paul Francis, Least of the Poor of Jesus', he adds the following postscript: 'Regarding Paolo [Sardi] and the other one, I have told them to do as God inspires them. As for myself (I say this with all my heart) I am quite indifferent, knowing for certain that all will be God's will. I said to Paolo when he spoke to me about whether I wish to write about him or not: just put all in the hands of God and have no doubts. *Deo Gratias.*'[28]

The bishop was far less enthusiastic than Paul about the idea of gathering companions to form a new religious community. If anything, there were too many religious orders and various attempts had been made by popes to limit their number. Nor were kings and governments always in favour of the creation of new religious groups. While it was relatively simple for a bishop to give someone the status of a hermit looking after a little chapel, it was quite another thing to allow the setting up of an Order or Congregation. Added to that, in the current climate of religious enthusiasm brought about by Paul's ministry, Bishop Gattinara probably thought it better to wait and see how things would develop.

Paul's Lenten 'campaign' concluded in Holy Week, during which he held a penitential procession. Among those who took part was the Marchesa Marianna della Scala del Pozzo, who walked barefoot, clothed

The chapel of the del Pozzo family at Retorto

in the black habit of a penitent. She admired the good work done by Paul and invited him to come and preach to the people who lived and worked on her husband's estates nearby, at Retorto and Portanova. Paul wrote to her, saying that he would come on the Tuesday of Easter week to begin his work there, as he would be kept busy at Castellazzo until then, because of the large number of people coming into the town for the Easter holidays. This letter began a correspondence which would last until 1738, as Paul became her spiritual director. At Retorto he held another penitential procession, in which he carried a large cross, now kept in the chapel on the estate.

Paul still felt called to go to Rome, so on 17 April 1721 the bishop wrote a letter of recommendation for him in which he described him as 'wearing a black habit of penance blessed by us; he is a young man of outstanding virtue and worthy of being kindly and charitably received wherever he may have occasion to present this letter.'[29] He made no reference to Paul's 'inspirations' or his Rule; the letter was valid for two months.

Unfortunately for Paul, Pope Clement XI had died on 19 March. This made a trip to Rome seem pointless, as there was no knowing how long the Cardinals would take to elect a successor. In fact, after what proved to be the shortest conclave of the eighteenth century, lasting only five weeks, Cardinal Conti was elected on 8 May, taking the name Innocent XIII.

Paul had decided to postpone his trip to Rome until after the summer. In the meantime, he set off, armed with the letter of recommendation, on his pilgrimage to Monte Verallo. According to Strambi, he wandered as far as the French border, looking for a home for himself and future companions.[30] In Turin he was seen on the street by the future Cardinal delle Lanze, at that time a ten year old boy, who found his austere, unkempt appearance quite frightening.

Towards the end of August, he went to Genoa, on the first stage of his trip to Rome. Here he stayed with the Marquis Paolo Girolamo Pallavicini, his friend from student days, who was kind enough to pay the cost of the sea voyage south to Civitavecchia. Before the ship set sail, John Baptist appeared on the scene and asked to come with him. When Paul refused to let him, his younger brother said,

'Go alone if you wish, but you'll have no peace without me',[31] and disappointedly went home to Castellazzo alone.

The voyage was uneventful until, on 8 September, the wind dropped and the boat was becalmed off the south coast of the Argentario peninsula. Monte Argentario, a mountain set in the sea and connected to the coast by two strips of land, had for centuries been a place favoured by hermits and those seeking to be alone with God. Paul gave this account of his first encounter with the mountain which was to be his home for many years:

On the feast of the Nativity of Our Lady the boat stopped near Monte Argentario; I did not disembark, but I ate some wild figs which the sailors had gathered on the land. However, standing on the boat, I fixed my eyes on the rocks and crags on the southern side of the mountain, and thought of withdrawing to one of those caves, and surely ending my days there.[32]

The next day the ship dropped anchor at Civitavecchia. Because of quarantine regulations, no one was allowed to leave the port for at least ten days. While waiting, Paul did not waste his time, taking the opportunity to offer religious instruction to his fellow passengers and writing out a clean copy of the Rule of the Poor of Jesus to present to the pope. Feeling perhaps a little remorse on account of his treatment of John Baptist, he wrote to him from Civitavecchia:

My dear brother in the Lord,

I arrived at Civitavecchia on 9 September in very favourable weather. I can tell you that I was hardly sick at all, except a little on the first day, and I made this trip with great spiritual fervour.

In my name, return thanks to the good God for it. I had such a brave heart that, for love of our dear Jesus, I would have gone to the ends of the earth. No fear ruled my heart.

When I'm in Rome I'll tell you everything in the hope that we may always be together, both in this earthly life and in heaven.[33]

The bay on the south side of
Monte Argentario in which Paul's ship was becalmed

When his quarantine was over, Paul set off on foot towards Rome, taking two days to cover the forty-five miles along the Via Aurelia from Civitavecchia to his final destination. He stayed overnight at an inn where his room was paid for by a fellow traveller, a Spaniard he had met on the way. The next day he reached Rome, coming first to St Peter's on his way into the city. He stopped there to pray but felt great desolation and aridity. He continued on towards the Tiber, which he crossed at the Ponte Sisto. It was a short walk from there to the Pilgrims' Hospice of the Trinità dei Pellegrini, where he would stay two nights.

St Peter's Square, Rome

The tradition of humble service of the poor, established there by St Philip Neri in 1549, still continued: Paul was amazed to have his feet washed by Cardinal Tolomei, a Jesuit, who also offered him a *testone*. Paul refused the coin, asking that it be given instead to a poor person. However, he accepted gratefully two loaves of bread, one of which he brought with him the next day when he set out to see the pope.

Pope Innocent XIII was staying at the summer palace on the Quirinal hill, known at that time as Monte Cavallo. Perhaps with the help of his now out-of-date letter of recommendation, Paul managed to get as far as the *Maestro di Camera*. In the midst of so much splendour the poor hermit must have looked a pitiful sight.

The Quirinal Palace, Rome

Unfortunately, there was no pity in the heart of the official who, on being told by Paul that he wanted to speak to the pope, promptly turned him out onto the street saying, 'Do you know how many loiterers come here every day? Be off with you!'[34]

How must this idealistic young man have felt after his first encounter with the papal court? Shocked at the treatment he had received, he crossed the piazza and sat down at a fountain in a nearby courtyard, intending to eat his one remaining little loaf. Strambi tells us that as he sat there, a poor man came up to him and asked for help:

On account of his youth and the disappointment he had suffered, Paul was feeling so hungry that three loaves would not have been enough for him; he could have eaten five if he had had them. But he went against himself and gave away half his bread for love of his God, whom by the light of faith he recognised in that poor man.[35]

His mission seemed to be a complete failure: thrown out of the palace, without a chance even to explain his business, much less present the Rule to the pope. Wandering down the hill, he saw the Basilica of St Mary Major, only about ten minutes' walk from the Quirinal, and decided to go there to entrust his mission to Mary.

Coming from the direction of the papal palace, Paul would have entered the Basilica from the door at the back of the building, between the main altar and the chapel of the *Madonna*, known as the Borghese Chapel. The cool stillness of the chapel had a soothing effect on him, as did the painting above the altar: the icon of Mary known as *Salus Populi Romani*, said to have been painted by St Luke. Kneeling there, allowing the turmoil to leave his heart, he prayed for understanding. Slowly he realised that it was not yet the time for presenting the Rule to the pope; that day would come. In the meantime, he must be faithful to the inspiration God had given him. When all doors seemed closed, the only way forward was to commit himself more fully to the work he had been given to do. Before the icon of Mary, he made a vow to promote the memory of the Passion of Jesus and to work to gather companions for this purpose.

NOTES

1. *Words*, 17.
2. *Ibid.*
3. *Ibid.*, 18f.
4. *Ibid.*, 19.
5. *Ibid.*, 19.
6. *Ibid.*, 14f.
7. *Ibid.*, 22.
8. *Ibid.*, 23.
9. *Ibid.*, 23f.
10. *Ibid.*, 14.
11. *Ibid.*, 28.
12. *Ibid.*, 30.
13. *Ibid.*, 32.
14. St Francis de Sales, *Treatise on the Love of God*, London, Burns & Oates, n.d., 310.
15. *Words*, 32f.
16. *Storia*, I, 194f.
17. *Ibid.*, I, 198.
18. *Ibid.*, I, 198.
19. *Words*, 43.
20. *Ibid.*, 44.
21. *Processi*, II, 11.
22. *Ibid.*, II, 31.
23. *Ibid.*, III, 7.
24. *Ibid.*, II, 76.
25. *Ibid.*, III, 214.
26. *Words*, 47.
27. *Ibid.*, 48.
28. *Ibid.*, 48.
29. *Storia*, I, 227.
30. *Vita*, 31.
31. *Ibid.*, 31.
32. *Processi*, IV, 315f.
33. *Words*, 51.
34. *Vita*, 39; *Processi*, IV, 316.
35. *Vita*, 39.

The Borghese Chapel in the
Basilica of St Mary Major, Rome

Chapter Three
(1721 – 1728)

The next morning Paul left the Hospice of the Trinity and walked to the *Ripa Grande*, where boats going down the river from the city were moored. Here he found one to take him as far as Fiumicino, on the coast. Another boatman then brought him on to Santa Severa and from there he walked to Civitavecchia. He had no money to pay the passage from Civitavecchia to Genoa, and besides, he did not want to go home without having a closer look at Monte Argentario. He set out on foot towards the north, staying overnight at Corneto (known today as Tarquinia) with the Augustinian friars, and at Montalto di Castro with a Corsican priest who lived there. He was travelling through the *Maremma*, the marshy region which would later be the scene of much of his missionary work. On the third night darkness came upon him when he was still out in open country, so he took shelter in a disused shepherds' hut. The next morning he found that his habit was covered with fleas; he had no change of clothing so, after trying to get rid of them, with only partial success, he had to continue on his journey with his new friends.

Unlike the countryside Paul had just passed through, the Argentario peninsula and the coastline beside it did not belong to the Papal States. The three towns of Porto Ercole, Porto Santo Stefano and Orbetello, together with Talamone further up the coast and Porto Longone, known today as Porto Azzurro on the island of Elba, were all part of the so-called Garrison State (*Stato dei Presidi*), which at that time belonged to Austria. For the moment this was not Paul's concern but, later, political and military questions would have consequences for his ministry in the area. At present, his aim was to discover if he could find a new home on the mountain since, after his failure in Rome, Bishop Gattinara was unlikely to change his mind about Paul gathering companions.

Arriving in Porto Ercole, Paul went to see the senior priest, Don Antonio Serra, who received him with great kindness and told him about an old hermitage on the mountainside two miles from the town. It was dedicated to Our Lady of the Annunciation. Paul decided to go and have a look at it and then go on to see the local bishop, after which he would go back to Castellazzo for John Baptist. After visiting the hermitage he set off for Pitigliano, the

Porto Ercole – Steps leading from the parish church to the harbour

cathedral town of the diocese, staying overnight at Orbetello with a religious community of Minims whose Prior would later become his confessor. When he arrived at Pitigliano, he discovered that the Bishop was at Pienza, thirty miles further inland. In the hot summer weather, fear of malaria drove those who could move away from the marshes to do so. Paul had already walked about forty miles from Orbetello, but he continued onwards. At Pienza, Bishop Fulvio Salvi received him and after hearing his request, gave him permission to live at the hermitage of the Annunciation.

From Pienza Paul walked to Pisa, where he found a boatman who was willing to take him on the canal to the coastal town of Livorno. At Livorno he stayed the night at the *Oratorio della Morte*; as he had nothing to eat, a Jew he had met begged some money with which he bought Paul food. At the harbour the captain of a cargo ship offered to take him to Genoa. The cargo was a load of animal skins; Paul was obliged to sleep on deck, on top of the skins. The journey was made quite unpleasant by the smell of the skins and, to add to his miseries, as they arrived in the port of Genoa, the captain shouted across to another ship owner that he had caught some of Paul's fleas, causing the sensitive young hermit to blush with embarrassment.

Paul had to stay on the ship to comply with quarantine regulations. These extra days spent in the harbour, sitting on the animal hides and still tormented by fleas, were almost too much for him. He became very discouraged and was almost ready to give up. Finally, he was allowed off the boat; no doubt he headed straight for the Pallavicini home to have a bath and wash his clothes.

On his return to Castellazzo, Paul went to see Bishop Gattinara to tell him about his adventures in Rome, his visit to Monte Argentario and his meeting with Bishop Salvi. He asked Bishop Gattinara to give John Baptist the black habit and to allow them both to go and live on Monte Argentario. The bishop agreed and, on the morning of 28 November 1721, in his private chapel, he clothed John Baptist in the black habit of a penitent, as he had done a year earlier for Paul.

The two brothers remained in Castellazzo until the following Lent, living at the hermitage of Santo Stefano. Meanwhile Paul wrote to Bishop Salvi asking for permission to bring a number of his friends with him when he would go to settle on Monte Argentario. The bishop replied that he should bring only one companion, since to form a community he would need approval from the pope.[1]

The worst of the winter weather over, Paul and John Baptist set out for their new home on the First Sunday of Lent, 22 February 1722. They carried with them a new letter of recommendation from Bishop Gattinara. The night before, Paul had written a long letter to his brothers and sisters in which he explained to them why he was going away:

Dearest brothers and sisters in Jesus Christ,

I, Paul Francis, poorest of men and a great sinner, your brother and unworthy servant of the Poor of Jesus Christ, must now (by divine order) leave this place in order to act upon inspirations from heaven. I am withdrawing into solitude to invite not only all rational creatures but also all non-rational and insensate creatures to keep me company in weeping over my grievous sins and in praising with immense love our dear God whom I have so often offended.[2]

The church and hermitage of Santo Stefano at Castellazzo

In the letter Paul went on to give his brothers and sisters what he called 'some spiritual advice', instructing them, as the oldest son, on their dealings with God and with people. On prayer he wrote: 'Do not let a day pass by without making half-an-hour or at least a quarter-of-an-hour's mental prayer upon the sorrowful Passion of the Redeemer. Do more if you can, but at least never omit this much. Constantly remember the pains of our crucified Love.'[3] On business matters he told them: 'Perform your tasks with good humour, with patience and humility. If you have debts, ask your creditors for the love of God to have some pity for you when perhaps you are unable to pay them. If someone owes you money, try to recover it but without recourse to law. Have compassion for everyone, especially the Lord's poor.'[4] He concluded the letter with the words, 'May God in his mercy bestow his blessing upon you all. Pray for me.'[5]

Paul and John Baptist went on foot to Genoa where they took ship to Civitavecchia. After the usual quarantine, they began the long walk north. On the evening of the Wednesday of Holy Week, 1 April, they reached Lake Burano, which was not far from their destination. This time Paul decided to avoid shepherds' huts so they slept in the open air, under a bush. When they woke up, there was a sprinkling of frost on their hair. They walked the remaining distance to Porto Ercole, arriving in time for the morning Mass. The archpriest, Don Antonio Serra, knew Paul already. He invited the two brothers to stay with him for the Easter Triduum.

Before taking up residence at the hermitage of the Annunciation, Paul and John Baptist thought they should go to Pitigliano to pay their respects to the bishop. On their way through Orbetello, they were stopped at the gate by soldiers and brought to be interrogated by the commander of the garrison, General Bartolomeo Espejo y Vera who, although a Spaniard, had taken the Austrian side in the War of the Spanish Succession. The Garrison States had been held by Spain since the 1530s until the Treaty of Utrecht in 1713 gave them, together with Naples and Sardinia, to Austria. The general, a devout man, was just coming out of the *Duomo* where he had been attending Benediction of the Blessed Sacrament. When asked by him who they were, Paul and John Baptist said, 'We are

The main door of the Duomo of Orbetello

two brothers who feel inspired by God to do penance on Monte Argentario.'[6] Satisfied that they were not spies disguised as hermits, he let them continue on their way to Pitigliano.

Returning from their meeting with the bishop, they went to the hermitage of the Annunciation. A former Augustinian monastery, it was a large building with five rooms on the ground floor and five upstairs. Although the structure was sound, conditions were primitive: John Baptist slept on a table but Paul, who was afraid of falling off, slept on the floor of the chapel, which was less rough than that of the hermitage. Their days were spent in prayer and study. They would rise at midnight for Matins and meditation, which lasted about three hours; in the morning they would be wakened by the drums of the soldiers in the fortress of Monte Filippo below. According to Strambi, 'There was continual silence; they spoke little to each other so as to be able to speak more with God and listen to his voice. The entire mountain and everything to be seen on it were for them an ever-open book, and a school for admiring more and more and praising the divine Creator.'[7] They fasted every day and depended for food on the free offerings of the people, as they had done at Castellazzo. Because they were living in such a solitary place and were not well known at first, there were times when they had nothing to eat except the few edible plants and herbs which were growing wild on the mountain. On Sundays they taught catechism in the small towns on the coast, John Baptist at Porto Santo Stefano on the north side of the lagoon and Paul at Porto Ercole on the south side; they would go through the streets ringing a bell and inviting the people to come to the church.

Apart from a short visit to Castellazzo to help a member of their family who seems to have been in some kind of morally dangerous situation, they stayed at the hermitage of the Annunciation for just over a year. Then one day they received a letter from Bishop Carlo Pignatelli, who had recently been appointed to the diocese of Gaeta, between Rome and Naples, inviting them to come and work in his diocese. How the bishop came to hear about the Danei brothers remains a mystery. It was possibly from Antonio Schiaffino and Michelangelo Michelini, the two young men about whom Fr Columbano had written to the Bishop of Alessandria; they were now living near Gaeta, at the hermitage of the *Madonna della Catena*. Bishop Pignatelli may also have heard of Paul and John Baptist from one of the army or navy officers, as Gaeta was also a port of strategic value for the Austrian forces in Italy.

Paul and John Baptist accepted Bishop Pignatelli's invitation and left Monte Argentario for Gaeta with a testimonial letter from Bishop Salvi in which he describes them as two brothers 'wearing the habit of hermits, a rough woollen tunic, with neither staff nor cloak, ...who go barefoot and bareheaded, even when travelling, who lead a life which is contemplative and active for the good of their neighbours, and who are known as the Poor of Jesus.'[8]

A summer morning on Monte Argentario

On their arrival, Bishop Pignatelli received them in his palace in the company of his secretary, Don Tommaso Perrone. The secretary, who was only twenty years old, was very impressed by Paul and John Baptist. He noted that they carried their breviaries 'in little leather bags hanging from their belts' and used them as pillows when sleeping on the floor.[9] The bishop suggested that they should live at the *Madonna della Catena* where, as well as their friends from Castellazzo, there were already some other hermits. He asked them to teach catechism to the people and to give pastoral assistance to the dying. Paul gave himself wholeheartedly to this latter work in particular and was often called out in the middle of the night to go and pray at the bedside of those in their last agony. The bishop had great confidence in Paul and, during Lent, invited him to preach in the crypt of the cathedral. He also asked him to preach the spiritual exercises to the candidates for ordination, for which he was criticised by many of the clergy because Paul himself was not a priest.

The young secretary, Don Tommaso, became very close to the two brothers and for a time thought seriously about joining them. He would often go to see them at the hermitage, sometimes staying overnight. He brought them with him to Naples to witness the liquefaction of the blood of Saint Januarius and to spend a few days at his family home. Paul gave him the Rule to copy, as it seemed as if he would embrace their way of life. However, Don Tommaso realised that such an austere life was not for him and gave up the idea, while remaining their good friend and doing whatever he could to advance their cause.

In 1724 Paul and John Baptist were invited to Troia by Bishop Emilio Cavalieri, the uncle of St Alphonsus de Liguori. Bishop Cavalieri was a member of a congregation of priests known as the *Pii Operai* ('Devout Workers'). He had been made Bishop of Troia at the age of thirty-one, having refused two years earlier; he was now sixty-one years old. He had heard about their way of life and the good work they were doing and was particularly interested in their desire to practice continual adoration of the Blessed Sacrament. He had tried to found a congregation in his diocese for the work of preaching missions, but the Dominican priest who had been

Pope Benedict XIII

helping him had died and so he was unable to set up the congregation. He thought that perhaps the two brothers might be interested in this work.

Paul and John Baptist stayed at Troia for six months, living in the bishop's palace. They must have looked, and felt, quite out of place and no doubt they longed to return to their solitude. Bishop Cavalieri asked them to go out at night to preach in the public squares of the town. He preferred to send Paul to those parts of the town which were known to be places of prostitution and immorality because, as he said, Paul was less faint-hearted and had a stronger voice. He arranged for some of the members of one of the local confraternities to go with him in case of any trouble.

While staying with Bishop Cavalieri, the two brothers made a pilgrimage to the shrine of St Michael the Archangel at Monte Gargano. As they prayed there, John Baptist heard the Lord say to him, 'I will visit you with a rod of iron and I will give you the Holy Spirit.' Years later when telling others about the words he heard, he commented, in an uncharacteristic moment of levity, 'The rod of iron we've had, but we're still waiting for the Holy Spirit.'[10]

The bishop, who was a doctor of canon and civil law, offered to revise the text of their Rule with them. He made a number of helpful suggestions, some of which came from the constitutions of the *Pii Operai*. He also advised them that it would be easier to have the Rule approved, and to carry out the kind of pastoral work they had in mind, if they were to become priests.

On 29 May 1724, while Paul and John Baptist were still at Gaeta, a new pope had been elected. A member of the noble and powerful Orsini family, Benedict XIII had entered the Dominican Order against his mother's wishes at the age of eighteen. She retaliated by having him made a cardinal when he was twenty-three, this time against his wishes. Before becoming pope, he had been Archbishop of Benevento for thirty-eight years, where he had been recognised as the opponent of any form of corruption among the clergy and a tireless worker for the reform of religious and the care of the sick and needy. When elected pope he was seventy-five years old. The historian Owen Chadwick describes him as follows:

Benedict XIII was a true friar. His face was stern and ascetic. He refused to be carried into St Peter's but went on foot. He continued to treat the Dominican general as his superior and kissed his hand. He refused to use the papal apartments in the Vatican and for a time occupied simpler and smaller rooms until he built himself a hermitage with whitewashed walls and without a view. At meals several times a week he waited on thirteen poor men. He personally visited hospitals, accepted invitations to consecrate bishops or churches, heard confessions, sometimes taught the catechism to a class of little children. He was a truly good pastor.[11]

The new pope declared 1725 a Holy Year and began his work of reform by convoking the Roman Provincial Council for 15 April 1725. Bishop Cavalieri would have liked to attend but was unable to do so because of ill health. When Paul and John Baptist expressed a wish to go to Rome for the Holy Year, he gave them a sheaf of letters of introduction to help them gain papal approval for their Rule. When the two arrived in Rome, they met Bishop Pignatelli and Don Tommaso Perrone who were there for the Council, and who invited the brothers to stay with them until they could find other accommodation.

The most significant meeting Paul and John Baptist had during their visit to Rome happened not as a result of Bishop Cavalieri's letters but purely by chance. As they were walking down the *Via delle Quattro Fontane* they were seen by a young Canon of St Peter's who wondered who they were. Some time later they went to the Vatican Basilica and were praying at the tomb of St Peter when the same canon happened to come by. Overcome by curiosity, he stopped to speak to them. He was Monsignor Marcello Crescenzi. At thirty years of age he was just a few months younger than Paul; he would become Paul's most faithful friend and greatest benefactor. Almost twenty years later, when he was Nuncio in Paris, he wrote to Paul recalling their first conversation:

When I saw you and your brother in the austere habit of penance, barefoot, standing praying at the confessio of the Holy Apostles, I had such a desire to speak to you and to find out who you were and what way of life you followed that I asked you lots of questions in the very

St Peter's Basilica, Rome: The Confessio

church itself; so it was that we became acquainted with one another and that afterwards I introduced you to Cardinal Corradini and to Pope Benedict XIII who later ordained you to the priesthood. The source of so much good, then, was your visiting those holy places dressed in that habit.[12]

It was Monsignor Crescenzi, as we read in his own words, who introduced Paul and John Baptist to Cardinal Corradini and who arranged with the cardinal for them to meet the pope. Cardinal Corradini was the Prefect of the Congregation of the Council, the office in the Roman Curia which had been set up to implement the decrees of the Council of Trent and which, by the eighteenth century, had become 'the most formidable of the Roman dicasteries'.[13] He belonged to the group of cardinals known as the *Zelanti*, those who were committed to the reform of the Church and wanted to protect the papacy from undue influence by governments. He had been a strong candidate in the two previous conclaves, and at the conclave which was to follow the death of Benedict XIII he would receive at one stage thirty out of a total of fifty-three votes. One of Cardinal Corradini's great concerns was the care of the underprivileged and he was at that time planning to build a new hospital in the Trastevere district of Rome for the treatment of leprosy and contagious diseases. Having met the two brothers at Monsignor Crescenzi's suggestion, he arranged for them to be presented to the pope on the afternoon of Monday, 21 May 1725. The occasion was a visit by Benedict XIII to the church of *Santa Maria in Domnica*, popularly known as *la Navicella* because of the boat-shaped fountain outside the church; he was to look at restoration work being carried out in the church under Corradini's supervision. Pope Benedict arrived in his carriage from the Lateran and attended vespers in the church. As he came out, Paul and John Baptist were waiting in the porch. They knelt before the pope and asked him for permission to gather companions to live and work with them. Without any hesitation, Pope Benedict granted their request *vivae vocis oraculo*, that is, verbally.

Having received the permission they were looking for, the two brothers decided to leave Rome and return to Gaeta. As Bishop Cavalieri later told them, it would have been better to have received something in writing, even a letter from some cardinal who had witnessed what happened.[14] Paul had not thought of this; he had been happy enough that the pope had expressed himself in favour of what he felt inspired to do and had given his blessing to him and his brother.

Bishop Cavalieri continued to write to them, asking them to return to Troia, but his idea was that they should found a new congregation which would be under the control of the local bishop; this was not what Paul had in mind. He and John Baptist decided to try to set up a community at the *Madonna della Catena* in Gaeta. Bishop Pignatelli sent them a young cleric, Nicola Tommaso Ricinelli, to act as bursar as they did not want to have to handle money or get involved in the material running of the hermitage. However, Paul and John Baptist's attempt to found a community there was unsuccessful and they had to go elsewhere. The two reasons for this failure seem to have been the unwillingness of the other hermits who were already there to adopt the Rule Paul had written and the fact that the church and hermitage were not under the direct control of the bishop because they were privately owned and endowed. Antonio Schiaffino seems to have contributed to these difficulties by trying to turn both the hermits and the church's patrons against Paul.

Monsignor (later Cardinal) Marcello Crescenzi

The Navicella fountain
with the church in the background

Fr Columbano, the Capuchin, had mentioned in his letter to Bishop Gattinara that Schiaffino also felt called to found a religious community; these aspirations seem to have led him to stir up opposition to Paul and John Baptist.

As a temporary measure, the two brothers moved from Gaeta to the sanctuary of the *Madonna della Civita* at Itri, a little to the north. This property was even more tied up by patronage than the one at Gaeta, so Paul knew there was no prospect of settling there. Here he met a local priest, Don Erasmo Tuccinardi, who became his confessor for a while and with whom he kept up correspondence for some years.

Wrought-ironwork on the gates of the church of the Navicella

'The Love of God': emblem above the door of the hospital of San Gallicano, Rome

Where was he to go now? Things had not worked out at Gaeta, nor were there any prospects at Troia, since Bishop Cavalieri had just died. At Monte Argentario they could live as hermits again but the bishop was against their having companions. Paul decided that they should return to Rome. During their last weeks there earlier in the summer, they had stayed with Don Emilio Lami who was to be the Prior of the new hospital in Trastevere; he had told them that there was a place for them there if they wanted it. On 21 September 1726 Paul wrote to Don Erasmo Tuccinardi:

> *Here we are safely arrived in Rome, thanks be to God. We shall have no further journey to make for God has arranged otherwise. We are staying at the Hospital which seems to us more suited to our purpose of being totally sacrificed to God's love. We have not yet had the formal opening. Within eight or ten days the Pope will consecrate the church. Then we shall go forward joyfully together to embrace our dear Jesus in the person of his poor.*[15]

On 6 October, feast of our Lady of the Rosary, Benedict XIII consecrated the church of the new hospital of San Gallicano; a side altar, dedicated to the Holy Family, was consecrated the same day by the Protector of the hospital, Cardinal Corradini. The cardinal entrusted the two brothers with the spiritual care of the patients. Within a short time, Paul organised catechism groups and began to prepare patients for Communion. In accordance with the constitution of the hospital, he and John Baptist took a vow of perpetual perseverance in the service of the sick.

Perhaps with the two brothers in mind, the constitution also made provision for those who were vowed to the hospital to be ordained as priests, which was what Corradini and Crescenzi thought Paul and John Baptist should do. On 15 March 1727 Paul wrote to Don Erasmo, 'The Superiors wish us to be ordained priests, continuing,

The Franciscan College of
San Bartolomeo on the Isola Tiberina

with the Pope's permission, in the same habit and life-style as at present.'[16] They were still wearing the black penitent's tunic and going barefoot. In their own minds they were following the original inspiration, but doing so at the hospital as no other way was as yet clear to them. Indeed, when Cardinal Corradini wrote to the Bishop of Alessandria for dimissorial letters for their ordination, he referred to them as 'Paul Francis and John Baptist Danei, two hermit brothers serving in the new hospital of San Gallicano.'[17]

Their theological studies before ordination were made at the Franciscan College of San Bartolomeo on the *Isola Tiberina*, ten minutes walk from San Gallicano; they attended classes given by Fr Domenico Maria da Roma. After a retreat at the Jesuit house of Sant'Andrea on the Quirinal, they were ordained subdeacons in the Basilica of St John Lateran on 11 April. Ordination to the diaconate followed on 1 May. They were ordained to the priesthood on 7 June by Pope Benedict XIII, having been presented to him as candidates by Cardinal Corradini. Monsignor Crescenzi and Don Emilio Lami attended the ceremony, which took place in St Peter's, in the Chapel of the Canons.

Twenty-nine candidates were ordained priests that morning; a further eighty-four received major and minor orders. The pope, by now almost eighty years old, insisted on doing the ordination himself. Many thought that Benedict XIII neglected political affairs and spent too much time at religious ceremonies. When on one occasion he was warned by someone close to him that he would kill himself with all these long ceremonies, he replied that a pope should die with his cope on his back.[18] That morning he spoke to no one after the ordination except the two hermits, asking them where they had received the other orders of subdiaconate and diaconate. In the hospital chapel the following day, Trinity Sunday, Paul and John Baptist celebrated Mass for the first time.

On 27 July their father, Luca Danei, died as a result of a fall. The journey to Castellazzo took them two months and when they arrived they were both suffering from malaria, because of which Paul was unable to celebrate Mass for eighteen days. Their visit was a great consolation to their family; it also gave them the opportunity to renounce their share of their father's inheritance. After a much quicker return journey, possibly paid for by the family, they arrived back in Rome on Sunday 26 October.

On their return from Castellazzo they learned that changes were being made in the running of the hospital which would make it difficult for them to remain there. In a letter to Don Erasmo, Paul explained their decision to leave the hospital:

We discovered that new Constitutions were being drawn up for the hospital and one of the principal treatments for those suffering from ringworm was blood-letting from the head. Although this is a work of great charity we hadn't the heart to do it, and in fact we were never required to do it. We were fully occupied in all other duties of charity, especially in the spiritual care of the sick, etc. – but never in this. We have seen His Eminence the Cardinal Protector, who to ensure proper discipline in the place and greater uniformity in the community required everyone to take part in the above-mentioned duty and in other works of charity (which I omit for brevity's sake). Since we had no heart for it (according to our way of doing it) His Eminence has very kindly procured a Brief for us from His Holiness to allow us to retire into solitude and to persevere in our own life-style, etc. And so it has turned out by God's grace.[19]

Paul's request to leave the hospital was dated 1 February 1728.[20] He and John Baptist had been there just a year and a half. Cardinal Corradini had been very understanding and had realised that the time had come for them to move on. He obtained a Brief from the pope[21] granting them a dispensation from their vow of perseverance at the hospital and giving them permission to celebrate Mass for one year. Every priest had to have what was called a title of ordination which determined where he ministered and where his income came from. Often a priest would receive the interest from a legacy assigned to the regular celebration of Mass in a particular chapel, or a similar benefice. He would then be considered as ordained for the service of that chapel. Religious were usually ordained under the title of poverty or 'the common table', which meant that their order undertook to provide for them. Paul and John Baptist had been ordained 'for the service of the hospital' of San

Gallicano, so when they left the hospital, the pope gave them permission to say Mass for a year, during which they would have to find a new title under which to exercise their ministry. John Baptist's health had begun to give cause for concern during their stay at San Gallicano as the 'fetid, stale air of the hospital' began to upset his stomach.[22] What really caused them to go elsewhere, however, was the increasing realisation that the work they were doing, while good in itself, was not really what God was asking of them; their deepest desire was to withdraw to a solitary place and live according to their own Rule. They decided that the best thing to do was to return to the hermitage of the Annunciation on Monte Argentario.

The Chapel of the Canons in St Peter's Basilica

NOTES

1. *Lettere*, I, 30.
2. *Words*, 52,2.
3. *Ibid.*, 53.
4. *Ibid.*, 55.
5. *Ibid.*, 56.
6. *Processi*, I, 49.
7. *Vita*, 48.
8. *Storia*, I, 284, n.4.
9. *Processi*, II, 91.
10. *Ibid.*, I, 52.
11. Chadwick, Owen, *The Popes and European Revolution*, Oxford, Clarendon Press, 1981, 292.
12. *Storia*, I, 305, n. 13.
13. Chadwick, *op. cit.*, 322.
14. *Storia*, I, 309.
15. *Words*, 63.
16. *Ibid.*, 65.
17. *Storia*, I, 347.
18. Chadwick, *op. cit.*, 292.
19. *Words*, 69f.
20. *Acta C.P.* (1931), 248f.
21. *Ibid.*, 248-251.
22. *Positio Ven. J. Baptistae*, 262, quoted in *Storia*, I, 363, n. 25.

Chapter Four
(1728 – 1737)

Paul and John Baptist returned to Monte Argentario at the beginning of March 1728. Bishop Fulvio Salvi had died on 23 May of the previous year. As yet, his successor had not been named so there was no point in their going to present themselves at the bishop's palace. Instead, they went first to Porto Ercole where they discovered that there was another hermit living at the hermitage of the Annunciation; it was Antonio Schiaffino. He too had been ordained to the priesthood since they had last seen him at Gaeta. Having encountered difficulties of his own at the *Madonna della Catena*, he had decided to move to the hermitage on Monte Argentario, which he had heard about from the Danei brothers. He had also drawn up a rule and was intent on gathering companions for a new religious congregation. Paul and John Baptist went up the mountain to meet him and asked if they could stay with him at the hermitage. Schiaffino became angry at the suggestion and chased them away from what was now his home, not theirs.

The two brothers decided that the best thing to do was to go back to Castellazzo. They walked down the other side of the mountain to Porto Santo Stefano where they found a boatman willing to take them on the first stage of their journey north. When they got into the boat, however, the wind dropped and the boat was unable to move. They knelt down in the boat and prayed for guidance; perhaps God did not want them to leave Monte Argentario after all. They decided to stay and when they disembarked, the boat was able to move again.

On making enquiries, they found out that there was another hermitage, dedicated to Sant'Antonio Abate (St Anthony of the Desert), on the east side of the mountain, looking towards Orbetello. It was small and in a very bad state of repair, but it was sufficient for their needs. With the permission of the archpriest of Porto Ercole, they settled there.

Within a few days, on 8 March, the parish priest of Monsindoli, Don Cristoforo Palmieri, was appointed Bishop of Soana and Pitigliano. The new bishop was content to let them stay at Sant'Antonio and, after hearing their story about meeting the pope at the *Navicella* and seeing the Apostolic Brief, he allowed them to welcome others who might want to join them.

A fisherman from Porto Ercole braves the open sea

Paul wrote to Don Erasmo Tuccinardi in October of the same year, 1728, to tell him about their new home which, he said, was 'most suitable for seeking the highest perfection', being very far from the town.[1] It was, he continued, 'a small Retreat with only two rooms and the church; but the recollection and holy silence here would keep us in peace even if we were a hundred.' In the same letter he told Don Erasmo about their first new companion, 'a good layman who is dressed as we are and looks after all the other things necessary for our vocation.' His name was Marco Arpeo, but he wanted to be known as Fra Giovanni Maria. Unfortunately, he did not stay.

Monsignor Crescenzi in Rome, who had been informed by Paul of their new situation, wrote on 13 March of the following year:

Roses blooming
at the hermitage of Sant'Antonio

I was delighted to hear that, with the Lord's help, you have arrived in good health at that much desired place of solitude, in which I hope you will not forget to pray for me... I am persuaded that in solitude you will find that peace which perhaps you were unable to have at the Hospital of San Gallicano, because of all the jobs you had to do there. I am very happy for you and I pray you to remember me in your holy sacrifices. I remain always willing to help you.[2]

Paul was full of hope for other companions, including perhaps Don Tuccinardi, but the few who came were not strong enough to remain.

In May 1730 their brother Antonio arrived at the hermitage. He had been sent by the family to find out how they were. Now twenty years old, he arrived 'dressed like a grand gentleman'[3] but was so struck by the way his brothers were living that he gave away his fashionable outfit, was clothed in the black habit and remained at the hermitage. In a letter to Tuccinardi, Paul said that Antonio had already completed his basic studies and that before receiving the habit he had made a retreat 'with the greatest possible devotion', after which he had embraced their way of life most willingly. He told Tuccinardi, 'He has the ability to do well and he makes me hopeful that he will be a successful worker "in the vineyard of the Lord of Hosts".'[4] Antonio was to remain several years in the Congregation founded by Paul and, after his ordination to the priesthood, become an excellent missionary. He was, however, unable to cope with the solitary aspect of the way of life of the community and, with the passage of time, found this more difficult to bear. He was dismissed by Paul in November 1742 but was re-admitted in September of the following year, apparently strengthened by the experience. Almost twenty years later, in 1761, his old difficulties surfaced again and he asked permission to leave the Congregation. He returned to Castellazzo where he lived a long and devout priestly life. With his sister Teresa and his brother Joseph, he acted as a witness at the Process of Canonisation of his brother Paul.

During the years spent at the hermitage of Sant'Antonio a number of other candidates joined the community but none of them stayed. There were only two rooms there and if people were to join the

The kitchen of the hermitage of Sant'Antonio

community, more space would be needed. Paul began to think about building a new house in which there would be room not only for a larger community but also for people who might want to come there to spend some time in prayer with the community or to make a retreat. The house itself would be called not a monastery or priory but a Retreat, a name used for their houses by certain communities devoted to solitude and austerity of life. For the present, however, he did not see how this might come about.

One of those who came to try out the life at the hermitage left a description of how Paul and his companions spent their day:

After I was clothed in the habit, we were living in the hermitage of Sant'Antonio. We were five in all: Fr Paul, Fr John Baptist, their brother Fr Antonio, who was a cleric, Brother Giovanni Maria and myself. Our style of life was as follows.

The hermitage consisted of a little church and two rooms, one below and one above with its own entrance. We all slept in the upstairs room on little sacks of straw placed on wooden boards, raised slightly off the stone floor. The sacks were separated from each other by curtains, so that we could not see each other. We would rise at midnight and go to the church where Fr Paul and his two brothers would recite Matins and I would say the rosary or other prayers with the other lay brother, my companion. When Matins was finished, we would all spend an hour in mental prayer. When our time in Choir was over, those who wished to return to rest did so, and the others occupied themselves in study or some other praiseworthy activity; in the morning, before daybreak, we would get up again and return to the church to say Prime and Tierce from the Divine Office, followed by another hour of mental prayer. Then the priests would celebrate holy Mass; after a period spent in thanksgiving, they would spend some time in the room below reading or writing. Then Fr Paul and Fr John Baptist would take their writings and go off separately into the woods, and sometimes Fr Anthony would do the same. We, the two lay brothers, would stay behind and do other jobs, such as working in the little garden there, gathering wood, or cooking a few herbs or vegetables in a hut facing the door of the hermitage, which served as our kitchen... An hour before midday, everyone returned to the hermitage and went

Monte Argentario.
A tree under which Paul used to
sit and read

to church to say Sext and None, after which we would go and have something to eat. This would consist of various types of bread, received as alms, a little wine with lots of water added, a soup made from herbs or vegetables, and a little dish of fish, which we had received in charity. After the meal we would spend a little time in recreation, either in the lower room which we used as a refectory or in the hut where we did the cooking. Then, after first saying Vespers, each would take his writings and go off to a secluded place as before. They would come back at about five o'clock in the evening to recite Compline, after which we would all spend an hour in mental prayer and then say the Rosary. In the winter, some hours would be devoted to study, after which we would take collation, since fasting was observed every day, unless it was a Feast day.[5]

Since their return to Monte Argentario in 1728 the two priest-hermits had been teaching catechism and hearing confessions in the nearby towns of Porto Ercole, Porto Santo Stefano and Orbetello. Towards the end of 1730 a new field of apostolic ministry was opened up to them when Bishop Palmieri asked them to preach a series of missions in his diocese. Missions were extremely popular in the eighteenth century and served as a special opportunity for catechesis and spiritual renewal, particularly in remote or neglected areas. Places such as the Tuscan *Maremma* were neglected not because there was a shortage of priests, but because the more capable priests were often unwilling to work in poor or unhealthy regions. In spite of the fact that between one and five per cent of the population were clerics, very few priests were committed to pastoral activities. In eighteenth century Italy there was a 'plethora of clergy who often could not be used for the cure of souls, who survived on a personal *patrimonio sacro* and who often searched for benefices, religious services and endowments provided by either the piety of the faithful or the interest of private families.'[6] Bishops of rural dioceses saw parish missions as a way of dealing with the religious ignorance of the people committed to their care and of giving them opportunities of spiritual guidance and the Sacrament of Reconciliation.

This new ministry opened up many possibilities for Paul. From now on, he and John Baptist would leave their solitude for extended

Pulpit used by Paul in Porto Ercole

periods of time, going from place to place, at first in their own diocese but very soon throughout the whole region of the *Maremma*. This brought Paul into contact with young men interested in pursuing a religious vocation in his community, with lay people willing to support the community's projects and later with bishops anxious to have a group of apostolic preachers based in their dioceses. More importantly, it was a means for him to reach out to thousands of people who were in need of the most basic pastoral care, enabling him to devote his life to those he had thought of during his retreat at Castallazzo as 'the many souls who do not experience the fruit of the Passion of my Jesus.'[7]

The first mission given by Paul and John Baptist was at Talamone, on the coast to the north of Orbetello, in December 1730. Among those who attended the mission was a twenty-seven year old woman from Orbetello whose name was Agnes Grazi. Her life was changed by Paul's preaching and, as a result of the impact his words made on her, she gave up her other interests and devoted herself primarily to prayer. Paul became her spiritual director and guided her to a high degree of mystical prayer. Agnes died in 1744, assisted in her last illness by Paul and his companions. One hundred and

sixty-five letters of spiritual direction written to her by Paul have been preserved.

At the beginning of 1731, as Paul was walking one day on the mountainside, he stopped to look across the lagoon towards the town of Orbetello. He knelt for a moment to pray, adoring the Blessed Sacrament in the main church of the town, the *Duomo*, which he could make out in the distance. He continued his prayer by saying the Litany of the Blessed Virgin Mary. As he prayed there, in the shade of an olive tree, the inspiration came to him that this was the spot on which he should build the new Retreat.

To build on this site, known as the Property of St Antonine, he would need the help of the people of Orbetello. He already knew some influential people in the town, including the family of Agnes Grazi, whose father was captain of the garrison. When he spoke to the Grazi family about it, they agreed to give him their support. Paul then made a formal request to the council for the property. The council was in favour but before they could give the property to Paul and his companions, a complicated series of negotiations had to be undergone because while the Property of St Antonine belonged to the people of Orbetello, the revenue from it did not, as it was a benefice of the Prior of Orbetello. The council was willing to give the prior sixteen ducats a year in compensation, but in order to do this they would need the permission of the Holy See, the correct procedure being that the request be made at Rome on their behalf by their Ordinary, Cardinal Lorenzo Altieri. As Abbot of Tre Fontane in Rome, the cardinal was the ecclesiastical superior of Orbetello which was not in the Diocese of Soana and Pitigliano but was a dependency of the Abbey of Tre Fontane.

The difficulties inherent in this strange juridic situation were added to when the council offended the cardinal: after writing to him about their intentions, they also made a direct approach to the Holy See instead of waiting for him to do so on their behalf. Paul had sent a letter to the cardinal on 19 July explaining the project and inviting him to contact Bishop Pignatelli, Cardinal Corradini and Monsignor Crescenzi for references. He then made this request: 'We, your humble servants and subjects, kneeling at your feet, beg Your Eminence to take this project under your paternal care if you think it will redound to the greater glory of God and the good of souls.'[8] Paul also wrote to Crescenzi, asking his support. However, Cardinal Altieri was not to be won over so easily. A contemporary described him in these words: 'He is of a melancholic nature, of few words and little literature... completely timid who, lest he make a mistake, delays decisions without any reason.'[9]

During the winter of 1731-32, some of Paul's supporters de-cided to measure out the piece of land intended for the new Retreat. When they did so, they discovered that the site of the building was not actually on the Property of St Antonine; it was on territory con-trolled exclusively by the civil authorities. This meant that the land could be transferred without the permission of the Holy See. How-ever, the cardinal's permission would be required before the land alongside the site of the Retreat could be given to Paul for a garden, since that was on the Property of St Antonine.

On 31 March Paul had occasion to write to the Bishop of Alessandria to request dimissorial letters for the ordination of his youngest brother, Antonio. In the letter, written from the hermitage of Sant'Antonio, he speaks about the building of the Retreat:

God's mercy is arranging for a Retreat of Penance to be built for us and our companions upon a property held by the city of Orbetello. It consists of a church dedicated to the Presentation of the Blessed Virgin Mary (a day of special blessing for us as the day we entered upon our present way of life) with about eighteen small, poor rooms, etc. Besides this a retreat house will be built, not only for priests of the neighbouring dioceses (for in the bad climate of this marshy locality hardly any have a seminary), but also for laymen who at convenient times would like to come here for spiritual exercises. A large quantity of material is already on the spot and the foundation-stone will be laid very shortly. I am telling you all this as to our own pastor, to recommend this holy work to your prayers and also to those of your beloved flock. This Retreat is being built here on Monte Argentario, close to where we are... When the Retreat is built, I hope that God's mercy will give us the grace to depend upon poverty, especially when others come. Already there are some who wish to do so, but we cannot receive them because we have no room.[10]

By the following April the problem with the cardinal was still unresolved. Apparently, he had said that he needed to have more information. Paul wrote to him from Porto Santo Stefano, where he was giving a mission, telling him politely that he had already told him all there was to tell and summarising what he had already written to him. He concluded: 'I abandon this affair into the hands of God; he knows the great needs there are in these parts, the difficulties caused by the [lack of] education of the clergy and other major problems. Blessed be God.'[11]

Clearly Paul was finding it difficult to understand why the cardinal should be standing in the way of what he believed to be God's will. In the letter he had again told Altieri that he could ask Cardinal Corradini and Monsignor Crescenzi if he wanted information about him and the community, which at that time consisted only of the three Danei brothers, as the others had left. He also added to the list the names of Bishop Gattinara, now Archbishop of Turin, and Bishop Palmieri at Pitigliano. It appears that Altieri contacted the latter who, on 22 December, sent him a detailed account of the little community who, he said, lived on Monte Argentario 'doing voluntary pen-

The town of Orbetello seen from Monte Argentario

96

ance and leading a very austere life, which is to be admired but which could not be imitated without a special grace from God.' He went on:

They are priests who follow their own Rule, wearing a very rough black habit next to their bare skin…; they always go barefoot, with head uncovered. Living from what is spontaneously given to them, they observe a continual Lenten fast in the hermitage, and the little rest they have is taken on straw. They celebrate the Office in their little church, both during the day and in the middle of the night, and the remainder of their time they spend in mental prayer and study.

The senior of the group, Paul, ministers as a missionary with zeal and fervour, going from one diocese to another giving missions; this year he has given missions in my diocese and is now about to go to Piombino and other places in the Diocese of Massa, in this Province of Siena. His younger brother, John Baptist, goes with him and gives catechesis, preaches spiritual exercises to the clergy and hears confessions. Both of them do a great deal for the spiritual growth of the people both by their good example and by the word of God.[12]

The report from Bishop Palmieri seems to have put Cardinal Altieri's mind at ease sufficiently for him to invite Paul to preach a mission in Orbetello itself, beginning on 4 February 1733. This was a providential opportunity to re-create some enthusiasm among the townspeople for the building of the Retreat, since after the various delays, they appeared to have lost interest in the project. Before giving the Papal Blessing at the end of the mission Paul reminded the people of the resolutions they had made and of all the work they had done in obtaining the land, securing the necessary permissions from both civil and ecclesiastical authorities, and having building materials transported to the site. But, he went on to say, the same people of Orbetello had more or less forgotten the commitment they had made and had abandoned the work they had begun. The building materials they had brought were lying unused on Monte Argentario, being walked on by their cattle. The wood which had been piled up was now rotting in the rain, bullocks were walking on the tiles and the drain pipes, and the swallows were building their nests and the foxes their lairs on the heaps of stone. He concluded by saying that since the people had obviously changed their minds and did not want the Retreat to be built there, he and his community had decided to leave Monte Argentario and go elsewhere.[13]

These last words were enough to move Paul's hearers to action. As he was leaving the town, a deputation from the civil and military authorities blocked his way. They insisted that he must not think of going somewhere else. They would take care of everything; he was to leave the matter completely in their hands.[14] Paul went back to Monte Argentario and traced the plan of the house on the ground with a stick. Work began right away and the foundation stone was laid on 4 March.

The next day Paul left for Piombino where he was to give a course of Lenten sermons. He put John Baptist in charge of the work. Soon afterwards a problem arose because of the shortage of water near the building site. John Baptist called the others together and carrying a cross led them in procession up the mountain, praying as he went. When they had gone about a hundred metres, he told them to start digging; water began to gush forth from the spot. To this day, the water supply for the Retreat still comes from 'Father John Baptist's Spring'.

It was during this visit to Piombino that Paul gave his first retreat to contemplative nuns. This was at the Monastery of St Clare, where his preaching brought about the conversion of Sister Maria Cherubina Bresciani, who until that time had lived her religious life in a careless, half-hearted way. At the bishop's request, Paul agreed to become her spiritual director and was to direct her by letter for more than twenty years.[15] When he returned to Monte Argentario, he discovered that much progress had been made and the building was now as tall as himself.

In the middle of June Paul went to Naples on some business regarding the new Retreat. He was back at Sant'Antonio by 2 August. In Naples there was talk of war with Spain and Paul realised that in the event of war, the Spaniards would attempt to take back the Garrison State from Austria. On 14 December he wrote to Sister Maria Cherubina Bresciani: '...for quite some time there has been no way to send me any more letters because of the threat of the scourge of war and the siege of the Garrisons. Let us try to appease God offended by our sins. Poor Italy is ravaged and ruined: may God in his mercy be good to her.'[16]

In spite of the war, Paul continued his mission preaching right through 1734, while the seventeen year old Don Carlos, a younger son of the King of Spain, played his part in the War of the Polish Succession by marching south with his army to take possession of Naples, entering the city on 10 May. After taking southern Italy and Sicily, the Spanish forces were able to focus their attention on the Garrison State. In the spring of the following year, 1735, they advanced on Porto Ercole, laying siege to the fortress of Monte Filippo. The siege lasted twenty-nine days. Finally on 14 May the Spaniards, who had been shelling for days, hit the ammunition stores and destroyed the fortress, taking prisoner the one hundred and twenty remaining Austrian soldiers. They now had control of the port and were able to attack the capital of the Garrison State, Orbetello.

Paul had left Monte Argentario in March to preach at Santa Fiora where the previous September he had given a mission to the people

The Fortress of Monte Filippo

and a retreat to the Capuchin nuns. On his way home, he was stopped by a Spanish patrol near Talamone and after interrogation was brought to their general, Don Jaime Gusmán y Dávalos Spínola, Marquis de La Mina. The general was impressed by him and later, during the siege, sent for him to hear his confession and those of the other officers. Paul now found himself in a position where he was known to and trusted by both sides in the war and was able to pass from one camp to another, attending to the needs of the wounded and the dying and of those who had been taken prisoner, and at times interceding with the military commanders on behalf of those who had been condemned to death.

Surrounded on three sides by water and on the fourth by stout walls built many years earlier during the long Spanish occupation, Orbetello was not going to be taken easily. The Marquis de La Mina began building a platform for his artillery at the foot of Monte Argentario, below the site of the still unfinished Retreat, at a place called Terrarossa, on the edge of the lagoon. From there he intended to shell the town, killing soldiers and civilians alike until they surrendered. When Paul heard this, he went to the general and pleaded on his knees before him for the people of Orbetello. Naturally the

The Spanish Governor's Palace at Porto Ercole

101

general was reluctant to change his plans but when Paul persisted, he eventually gave in and agreed not to shell the town.

The garrison at Orbetello consisting of about eight hundred Austrian troops surrendered on 28 June. Don Jaime made his triumphal entry into the town on 20 July, but Paul was not there to witness it. Before the surrender of the town he had left with John Baptist for a series of missions on the island of Elba. It was during this journey that he met two future members of his community, both of whom he would direct by letter for a number of years before they were able to enter the Congregation: Francesco Antonio Appiani, a young nobleman whose father would oppose his embracing so austere a way of life, and Tommaso Fossi, destined to become the father of eight children and to enter the Congregation after the death of his wife when he was fifty-six years old.

Paul continued his mission preaching throughout the summer, returning to Sant'Antonio in September. During his absence, Anthony had been supervising the work on the new building. Paul wrote to Gregorio Gualas Y Puego, whom he had met on the island of Elba:

On my arrival here at Monte Argentario, I found a lime-kiln being constructed to finish the Retreat

Fr Fulgenzio (Pastorelli)

quickly. The latter was already half-built before the siege of the Garrisons but because of the siege it was never completed. On account of the losses suffered by the people of Orbetello during the siege I doubted whether it could be finished so quickly, but I now see they are determined to pursue the project of the said retreat.[17]

At Christmas a newly-ordained priest in his mid-twenties arrived to join the community. He was Don Fulgenzio Pastorelli, who had first met Paul in 1731 during a mission at Magliano. Of those who joined the Danei brothers on Monte Argentario, he was the first to stay.

Work on the future Retreat of the Presentation continued but was hampered by the lack of money after the war. It was probably the Marquis de La Mina who suggested that Paul should go to Naples to ask for help from Don Carlos, now King Charles III of Naples, since he had already given his 'royal assent' to the foundation. In January 1736, with the aid of a letter of introduction to 'one of the principal gentlemen of the court',[18] Paul and John Baptist were able to have an audience with the king. Charles III, who was at lunch, welcomed them with kindness and, after listening to their story, confirmed his approval of the foundation and gave them one hundred *doppie*, a considerable sum of money, to help complete the building of the Retreat.

Paul was back from Naples by the beginning of February. Don Jaime had been replaced by a new commanding officer, General Garma, who was just as well-disposed to Paul and his community as his predecessor had been. By October the walls and roof of the Retreat were finished but there was still work to be done. Paul wrote to Tommaso Fossi:

Were it not for lack of funds we would enter it on the feast of the Presentation, but we are short of timber to make doors and window-frames. If you could find a little for us there and also procure some in Marciana, it would be a great act of charity. It would then be our business to have it brought here provided we can find some one to manage a load of wood for us... Others wish to come [to join the community] but the retreat is not finished. What a help it would be to have a few planks of seasoned timber.[19]

The following summer everything was finished and both house and church were ready. Paul wrote to Cardinal Altieri for permission to have the church blessed as a public oratory. As before, the cardinal was uncooperative. He thought that it should be simply a private oratory, in which the priests of the community could say Mass without the people being able to attend. His vicar general at Orbetello, Giovanni Maria Moretti, pointed out that while the cardinal could authorise the church being opened as a public oratory, if he wanted it to be a private one, then the permission of the Holy See would be required if the priests were to be able to say Mass there.

In fact, the cardinal had still not given his consent for the transfer of ownership of the adjoining property. The previous year he had demanded to see the Constitutions of the new Congregation and had made a number of suggestions for altering them, particularly with regard to the Congregation's refusal to have benefices or other fixed sources of income. He said that Paul should not be unreasonable but should learn from the Jesuits, who had started out that way but had learned that it was just not practical. On that occasion, his vicar general, who supported Paul, had said that in his opinion this kind of absolute poverty was the principal distinguishing characteristic of the new Congregation.

Without Cardinal Altieri's permission to have the church blessed, the community, who were by now nine in number, would be obliged to walk more than a mile every morning from the new Retreat to the hermitage of Sant'Antonio in order to celebrate Mass. Paul did not want to move into the new house until the church was blessed but, as he explained to the cardinal, conditions in the hermitage were extremely primitive:

At present [we] are living in a poor hovel, so small and wretched that anyone who sees so many living in it is moved to compassion. The simple fact is that the four lay brothers sleep in a single hut; because the place is so small and the hot weather coming on, we are infested with a huge number of fleas and other filth and there is no way of dealing with them.[20]

Paul's description of the dreadful conditions in which the

The Retreat of the Presentation on Monte Argentario

community was living was not sufficient to speed up the cardinal's response. Nor was his declaration in the same letter that they wanted the church blessed so as 'to celebrate therein the sacred mysteries, to sing the praises of God day and night, to devote ourselves to prayer and study and thus qualify ourselves still more to assist our poverty-stricken neighbours, especially those of these wretched and forsaken *maremme*.'[21]

In all Paul wrote at least seven letters to the cardinal on this subject between the beginning of June and the end of August. However, he was not the only one in communication with Cardinal Altieri, as a number of people in Orbetello were opposed to the opening of the new church, particularly some priests and religious who were afraid that many would go there to Mass instead of to the churches in the town. Paul was very direct in telling Altieri of the scandal caused by his letting himself be guided by such people. He wrote to him on 15 August:

Let me tell your Eminence that yesterday I happened to be in Orbetello when one of the king's chief commanding officers asked me when would be the blessing of the church, which the king had so zealously helped [to build]. I tried to say what I could, as God inspired me, to give him the hope that this would happen soon. 'But', he said, 'why have you not received from the Court of Rome the assent of the king for the transfer [of ownership]?' Not knowing what to answer, I said, 'I believe that everything will turn out all right, because His Eminence, our Pastor, is all in favour of this work. But he replied, 'If you have not received the royal assent, you should write to the king to tell him that his royal approval has had no effect in Rome.' 'Sir', I replied, 'It isn't necessary to write to the king, nor should we do so, since the royal assent will have all the good effects [we are waiting for].' After this he added, 'Father Paul, do you know who doesn't want this work done? The priests and the friars, for fear that it will take away offerings from them; it's all accursed self-interest, and you should realise that the officials and the people know it, and they also know that, according to the Council of Trent, His Eminence the Lord Cardinal, as the Ordinary, can give the permission for the church to be blessed, and if he can do it, why doesn't he?'[22]

At this stage the cardinal agreed to the transfer of ownership and signed the necessary documents, but he would not give in on the question of the opening of the church. He advised Paul to write to the Holy See for permission to have it blessed as a private oratory. Reluctantly, Paul agreed to do so, writing to Altieri on 29 August: 'Seeing that on account of our faults we are unworthy to receive a favour which Your Eminence can so easily grant, we are now having recourse to the Apostolic See to obtain a Brief for a private oratory as Your Eminence has suggested, and we are content with that.'[23] However, both he and Altieri had reckoned without Paul's two good friends in Rome, Monsignor Cescenzi and Cardinal Corradini, who were handling the request on his behalf. On 31 August, before Paul's letter of submission would have reached Rome, they obtained from Pope Clement XII an Apostolic Brief for the church to be blessed as a public oratory, thus bypassing the unwilling Altieri and obtaining what Paul had wanted from the beginning. Even so, it would be another four years before Altieri would give them permission to reserve the Blessed Sacrament.

Two weeks later, in the presence of the civil and military authorities and a large number of people from Orbetello, including the Grazi family, Monsignor Moretti blessed the Retreat and church of the Presentation of the Blessed Virgin Mary and celebrated the first Mass in what Paul had described in one of his letters to Altieri as 'the most beautiful and seemly church in these parts'.[24] In a letter to Sister Maria Cherubina Bresciani, Paul gave his own account of what happened:

On 14 September, the day of the Exaltation of the Holy Cross, principal feast of our small and new-born Congregation, the solemn entry and blessing of the church and Retreat took place. I had the duty of leading the way with the cross aloft, and with a rope around my neck. Eight companions followed me, that is five priests including myself, and four lay brothers. A sermon was given suitable to the occasion and the function then concluded. All the above companions are wearing the same habit as myself; we are nine in all, besides another who wishes to take the habit. All serve God fervently except the unworthy one who is writing.[25]

NOTES

1. *Lettere*, V, 18.
2. *Storia*, I, 375.
3. *Ibid.*, I, 377, n.24.
4. *Lettere*, I, 82.
5. *Vita*, 65f.
6. Rosa, Mario, "The Italian Churches", in Callaghan, W.J. and D. Higgs, (eds.), *Church and Society in Catholic Europe in the Eighteenth Century*, Cambridge, University Press, 1979, 68.
7. *Words*, 22.
8. *Ibid.*, 77.
9. *Ibid.*, 78.
10. *Ibid.*, 79f.
11. *Lettere*, I, 358f.
12. *Storia*, I, 416.
13. *Ibid.*, I, 420.
14. *Ibid.*, I, 421.
15. *Lettere*, I, 436, n.1.
16. *Words*, 82f.
17. *Ibid.*, 99.
18. *Storia d. Fond.*, in *Bollettino* (1922), 346.
19. *Words*, 125.
20. *Ibid.*, 151.
21. *Ibid.*, 150f.
22. *Lettere*, I, 371f.
23. *Words*, 159.
24. *Lettere*, I, 370.
25. *Words*, 163.

Monte Argentario.
The church of the
Presentation of Mary

Chapter Five
(1737 – 1746)

The struggle surrounding the opening of the Retreat of the Presentation had been the focus of Paul's attention during 1737. With the building complete and the religious settled into their new home, he was able to devote more of his energy in the following year to the work of evangelisation, being occupied in preaching missions for much of the year. One of the main tasks of his community, now known as the 'Least Discalced Clerics of the Holy Cross and Passion of Jesus Christ', was still the teaching of prayer. Consequently, he was always insistent that a balance should be found between missionary activity and contemplative living in the Retreat. In the earliest complete text of the Rule which has come down to us, the text submitted by Paul to Cardinal Altieri in 1736, he explains how this is to be put into practice:

The order in which the brothers are to leave the house, and go out from solitude will be as follows: if, for example, there are twelve brothers capable of helping their neighbour, six of them will go out, two by two, or in larger groups if needed, to work in the dear vineyard of Jesus Christ, giving Missions and spiritual exercises, and doing other good works. The other six will remain at home, singing psalms and giving praise to God in prayer, and fasting. When the first six brothers return to solitude, worn out by their labours, the other six will go to work in the vineyard of God, while the first six remain in the holy solitude devoting themselves to prayer as above.[1]

Paul realised from his own experience and from his work with others that the only means to effective pastoral action was a living relationship with God. Given that the aim of the community was to be the promotion of the memory of the Passion of Jesus, only prolonged periods of contemplation would prepare the missionaries for their task. He wrote in the first chapter of the same text of the Rule:

Since one of the principal aims of this least Congregation consists not only in being untiring in holy prayer ourselves in order to attain union with God, but also in helping our neighbours, instructing them in the easiest way possible in this angelic exercise; therefore

Crucifix used by Paul when preaching missions

the brothers of this Congregation, who will be recognised as able, whether in time of Missions, or on the occasion of some other devout exercise, shall meditate aloud for the people on the divine mysteries of the most holy Life, Passion and Death of Jesus our true Good, doing this in time of Missions after the sermon, and in other times when it will be thought most appropriate, promoting this meditation also in the sacred tribunal of Penance, and in any other kind of spiritual conference, as the most effective means of destroying vice, and leading the soul in a short time to great holiness.[2]

One of Paul's main concerns now was to have the Rule approved by the pope. In November 1737, just after the opening of the Retreat of the Presentation, he had written to Sister Maria Cherubina Bresciani: 'Very shortly I must go to Rome to throw myself at the feet of the Supreme Pontiff for the approval of the Rule.'[3] He visited Rome at the beginning of 1738 and received an indult from the pope enabling him to preach anywhere in Italy as an 'Apostolic Missionary', but was unable for the present to make any progress with the Rule. Of the nine religious who had entered the new Retreat, most had now left. Critics were saying that the life was too severe and that because of this the pope was refusing to approve the Rule. In fact the pope was doing very little; he was in poor health and nearing the end of his life.

On 26 May 1739 Bishop Palmieri died; he had been a strong supporter of the Congregation and a good friend to Paul. A month later Paul received a letter from Monsignor Crescenzi telling him that he was leaving Rome, as he had been appointed Papal Nuncio in Paris. Cardinal Corradini was now eighty-one years old and Monsignor Crescenzi was unwilling to leave Rome without finding someone to take his place as Paul's guardian angel. He had recommended him and the little Congregation to the protection of the Venetian cardinal, Carlo Rezzonico, who was just a few months older than Paul. Crescenzi told Paul that he had given plenty of information to the Cardinal, whom he described as 'very upright and well-disposed towards your Retreat'. He assured Paul that he would always find him 'well-disposed and willing [to help you] when you are in need.'[4] Within less than a fortnight Cardinal Rezzonico him-

Rome. Fountain at the church of Santa Maria ai Monti

self had written to Paul telling him that he was ready to do whatever he could to help his 'holy Institute'.[5]

With the support now of two cardinals Paul thought that the time had come to seek approval for the Rule. However, Pope Clement died on 6 February 1740; the same day, Rezzonico wrote to him, saying that nothing could be done until after the election of the new pope.

The conclave which followed was the longest in modern history, lasting six months. After 255 ballots, the Archbishop of Bologna, Cardinal Prospero Lambertini, was elected, taking the name Benedict XIV. Exactly a week later, on 24 August, Paul wrote to Cardinal Rezzonico asking him to see what steps could be taken to have the Rule approved. On 14 September Paul lamented in a letter to Agnes Grazi that he had not received any reply from Rome 'from someone whom I hoped and believed would achieve a great deal.'[6] That very day, however, Rezzonico wrote to him telling him what he had done:

I did not want to reply to your letter of the twenty-fourth of last month without having first done something of service to the Retreat. Yesterday I was at the feet of His Holiness and I explained to him in outline the idea behind this holy Institute, the purpose for which it was founded, the great results you have achieved, and the growth you desire and would be able to have if your Constitutions were approved by the Holy See.

His Holiness listened with great satisfaction to everything I told him and gave it his approval. He told me to let you know that if one of you would come to Rome and bring the Constitutions you wish to have approved, he would hope to be able to give you what you seek and send you back to your apostolic labours without delay…

Furthermore, when you come to Rome, you and your companion can come to my house, where I will give you two rooms in which you can come and go as you please, and I assure you that they will be no poorer than the ones you have in the Retreat; you can attend to all your business, and indeed to your prayer life, without anyone bothering you. Please let me know what you decide about coming to Rome and about my offer of hospitality.[7]

Benedict XIV was ready to do what he could to help the new Congregation, not just because his trusted adviser Cardinal Rezzonico had suggested it, but also because he himself was always interested in the renewal of religious life. In this he showed a preference for those orders which united austerity of life with missionary activity directed towards the poor and neglected. As part of his efforts at pastoral renewal he also wrote letters on parish missions and the teaching of meditation to the laity. His enthusiasm for Paul's Rule, therefore, was not surprising.

On 1 October Paul wrote to Francesco Antonio Appiani that things were going very well in Rome and that as the pope had said that he was to bring the Constitutions to him, he would leave for Rome at the end of the month.[8] He arrived with John Baptist on 13 November and went to Rezzonico's residence, the Palazzo Altemps, near the Piazza Navona. When the two brothers were presented to the pope, he glanced through the text of the Rule they had given him and then said to them, 'This Congregation of the Passion of Jesus Christ should have been the first to be founded and it has arrived last!'[9] Benedict XIV set up a commission to examine the Rule (or Constitutions) consisting of Cardinals Rezzonico and Corradini and, as secretary of the commission, the *Abate* Count Pietro Maria Garagni.

Pope Benedict XIV

114

Like the Danei brothers, Count Garagni was Piedmontese. However, when Paul and John Baptist went to visit him in order to introduce themselves to him, he was horrified by their appearance and, after letting them know that he did not admire such eccentricities, he cut short the interview and more or less turned them out. That night he was unable to sleep; there was something troubling his conscience. As he lay awake trying to discover what it was, he suddenly remembered his treatment of the two brothers. He got up and called his servants, presumably thinking that if he was awake, they should be too. He told them that the next morning they were to go for Paul and John Baptist and bring them to him. The following morning, when the two arrived at his house, barefoot and clad in the rough black tunic as before, he greeted them warmly and proceeded to apologise for having treated them so badly the previous day. This incident won Garagni over to their side and began a lasting friendship.

Paul and John Baptist returned to Monte Argentario on 23 December, leaving the commission to complete its task. A few days after his arrival, Paul wrote to Count Garagni encouraging him in his work and expressing the hope that any revision of the Rule would not result in the religious being obliged to pastoral works other than Missions, which might necessitate their leaving that solitude 'in which the spirit [can] rest at the feet of the Crucified so as to be renewed and consoled by recollection and prayer, since our weaknesses and distractions upset our fragile humanity even when we are working for the good of our neighbours.'[10]

Paul continued to worry that in its revision of the Rule the commission might alter the spirit of the congregation and decided to write to each of the three commission members individually. His letter to Count Garagni, written on 10 January 1741, gives a wonderful summary of his understanding of the Congregation's role of promoting the memory of the Passion:

The most effective means of rooting out vice and planting true reverence is meditation on the most bitter pains of our Divine Saviour; and since the majority of the faithful live in forgetfulness of how much our most loveable Jesus has done and suffered, and because of this spend their lives sleeping soundly in the horrible quagmire of wickedness, zealous workers, poor in spirit and detached from all created things, are needed to waken them from this detestable lethargy, so that with the trumpet of the word of God and by means of the most holy Passion of Jesus Christ, they may waken those poor sinners who 'sit in darkness and in the shadow of death'[11]*, so that God will be glorified in so many converted souls and in many others who will devote themselves to learning how to pray and, in this way, to holiness of life.*[12]

The work of examining the Rule was delayed, partly because Cardinal Corradini, in spite of his age, was also working on a new Concordat with the Kingdom of Naples. Finally, on 15 May Pope Benedict XIV signed the document approving the Rules and Constitutions. The document in question was a Rescript, not an Apostolic Brief as Rezzonico had hoped, the difference being that a Rescript was effective only during the lifetime of the pope who granted it, whereas a Brief was still recognised after the pope's death. However, since the congregation had only one house and in that house only six people, which was half the number usually required for a religious house, it was an extraordinary achievement. In the Rescript, the pope gave the approval so that 'the members of the new Institute whose sole aim is giving missions' might work especially 'in remote and insalubrious regions, islands and abandoned places'.[13]

With the papal approval of the Rules and Constitutions, as they were now called, the community at the Retreat of the Presentation would be able to make their first public religious profession, as until now they had only had private vows. They would also be able to wear on their tunics the distinctive 'sign' of the Passion, revealed to Paul at Castellazzo more than twenty years before. Paul wrote to Count Garagni on 18 May expressing the hope that they might at last receive permission to reserve the Blessed Sacrament as they were about to make a 'solemn' retreat to prepare them for their profession of vows and, he went on, 'above all to dispose us for being signed with that most holy sign of salvation, which will show to all the peoples that we are destined to preach the most bitter pains

116

*Passionist Sign used by
St Paul of the Cross*

of our Jesus, promoting in all hearts the true devotion to the Passion, which is such an effective means for removing the many evils which are flooding our poor Catholic world...'[14]

On 30 May Canon Angelo di Stefano arrived at Monte Argentario to be received (for the second time) as a postulant. He had come from Rome and brought with him the rescript approving the Rules and Constitutions, given to him for Paul by his friend Garagni, and with it the permission to reserve the Blessed Sacrament, which Garagni had somehow managed to get from Cardinal Altieri. 'With these papers', wrote Garagni, 'I send you my heart, full of affectionate respect, assuring you that wherever I am able to serve you, I will always do so willingly and wholeheartedly as I have done, being sure that you will not forget to pray for me.'[15] Two days later, on the feast of Corpus Christi, the little community sang the *Te Deum* after Mass and then in the tabernacle which had lain empty for four years they placed the Blessed Sacrament.

At the end of the ten-day retreat prescribed by the Rules and Constitutions, six companions made their religious profession. In addition to the vows of poverty, chastity and obedience, they took the special vow to promote in the hearts of all the memory of the Passion of Jesus,

117

which Paul had taken after being thrown out of the papal palace on his first visit to Rome, twenty years earlier. They then received on their black habits the sign of the Passion, Paul placing it first on himself and then on the others. Each of them would no longer use his family name but would be known by a new surname, expressing for him a particular devotion to an aspect of the mystery of Christ or to a patron saint. The six who made profession that day were Fathers Paul of the Cross (Danei), John Baptist of St Michael the Archangel (Danei), Antonio of the Passion (Danei), Fulgenzio of Jesus (Pastorelli), Carlo of the Mother of God (Salemmi) and Brother Pietro (Cavalieri). On the same day Don Angelo received the habit but, unfortunately, he was to stay only until the following January, not being able for the life. The other younger man who received the habit with him was Brother Giuseppino of Mary (Pitruzello), who would be the first brother to persevere in the Congregation.

In a long letter to his former confessor, Canon Cerruti, Paul gave a very detailed description of the mission and lifestyle set out in the newly-approved Rule. He also described for him the habit worn by the members of the community:

> *The habit is a black clerical tunic of rough black cloth with a mantle which comes to the knees... On the tunic and mantle, on the left side of the breast, we wear the admirable and most holy sign of the Passion, which consists of a white cross planted in a heart, on which is written in white letters the name of our dearest Jesus, with the title of the most holy Passion, in accordance with the light so clear which I had about twenty-three years ago, as you know well, and which was made clearer to me by the Supreme Good by means of the aforementioned title: and the whole title is written in white letters (Jesu Christi Passio), which inspires great devotion.*[16]

With the approval of the Rule, critics of the way of life of the community on Monte Argentario were silenced and new members began to join. Among those were the first Swiss Passionist, Brother Giacomo of St Aloysius (Gianiel), and another priest for the community, Fr Marcaurelio of the Blessed Sacrament (Pastorelli). Born in Nice, Marcaurelio had been a member of a Congregation known

The walls of the town of Toscanella (Tuscania)

as the *Dottrinari*, devoted to the teaching of Christian Doctrine. He had been a professor of theology and also novice master, and brought to the new Congregation much experience in spiritual and theological formation, which he would use later in setting up structures for the noviciate and the houses of study.

By July 1743 Paul was able to write to Canon Cerutti of Alessandria: 'The Retreat is now full; there is no more room as all the cells are occupied.'[17] In the same letter he spoke of two possible new foundations, one at Toscanella (known today as Tuscania) and the other at Vetralla. Both were places where he had given missions and where the people would be happy to welcome a community of the new Congregation of the Passion. He had been trying since the approbation of the Rule to make a foundation on the island of Elba, having also made an earlier attempt at the beginning of the 1730s, but this had proved impossible. After a successful mission at Toscanella in January 1743 Paul had written to Count Garagni saying that he was trying to arrange the foundation of another house and that the people of Toscanella were 'frantic with the desire to give a church which is in solitude' to the Congregation.[18] However, even though the town council agreed to give the church of the *Madonna del Cerro* for this purpose in July 1743, for various reasons the foundation would not be made until 1748.

The most feasible place for a new foundation was Vetralla. Paul had given a mission there after Easter in 1742; this was followed by a retreat to the Carmelite nuns on the outskirts of the town. As a result of his preaching, the people of Vetralla offered him a Retreat at Monte Foligno, to be built at the expense of the town council. There was a chapel there, dedicated to St Michael the Archangel, with a little hermitage built alongside it. Of the group of hermits who had been there, only one was still living. He had no objection to the Congregation coming there. In order to proceed with the building of a Retreat on the hillside, the council needed the consent of the Congregation for Good Government, the department in Rome which was responsible for the administration of the Papal States. When the Capuchin friars of Vetralla heard that the council intended giving Paul the hermitage on Monte Foligno, they lodged an objection with the Prefect of the Congregation for Good Government, Cardinal Rivera, saying that the proposed foundation would interfere with their right to quest, that is, to go from house to house collecting money and other goods for the upkeep of their monastery. On the basis of their objection to what they saw as competition, Cardinal Rivera turned down the request of the council. Paul did not lose hope, but decided to wait until the following year.

In 1743, there was an extraordinary growth in the size of the community. The time had come to set in motion another attempt at the Vetralla foundation. Paul had lost two of his best friends at Rome: Cardinal Corradini had died on 8 February, and on 11 March Cardinal Rezzonico had been made Bishop of Padua. In spite of the distance, Paul kept Rezzonico in touch with what was happening, as he did also with Crescenzi who was still in France. On 6 May Crescenzi wrote to him from the Paris Nunciature: 'I too want some other houses of yours to be founded, but in the Papal States, so as to be more visible to the Court of Rome, in order that [the Congregation] might become better known, and may be even more esteemed on account of that austere, penitential life... to which the Lord has called you.'[19]

In August, acting on the advice of the Venerable Geltrude Salandri, for whose community at Valentano Paul had just finished preaching a retreat, he prepared a petition to the Congregation for Good Government. He had already written to them the previous year, explaining that the Capuchin friars had nothing to fear from the proposed foundation. This time he sent the outline of the petition to Garagni so that he could draw up the final text in the correct form and present it personally to the Congregation in Rome. He also had a copy sent to the Governor of Vetralla. Meanwhile Garagni was having meetings with Cardinal Alessandro Albani, a member of the Congregation for Good Government, and Monsignor Conti, its secretary, to interest them in the case. In October he wrote to Paul, advising him to come to Rome to meet those in the Congregation who would support him. Paul waited until after the feast of the Presentation of Mary, leaving for Rome on 23 November. He met Cardinal Albani, Cardinal Rivera, Prefect of the Congregation for Good Government, Cardinal Valenti, Secretary of State, and Cardinal Colonna-Sciarra, the new Abbot of Tre Fontane. He was delighted to meet his old friend Marcello Crescenzi, who had recently been recalled from Paris and made a cardinal. He also had an audience with the pope. The result was that at the end of December, with the encouragement of Cardinal Rivera, Pope Benedict XIV instructed the Congregation for Good Government to grant the request of the town council of Vetralla and let the new foundation go ahead. Permission was also granted for the proposed foundation at Toscanella. Paul wrote to Garagni on 22 January 1744 to thank him for all he had done.

Count Garagni had in fact done more than smooth out the difficulties for the foundation at Vetralla, for in doing so he had opened up the possibility of another foundation, which would in fact be made before that of Toscanella. When he told Cardinal Alessandro Albani about the desire of the council of Vetralla to establish a house of the new Congregation on Monte Foligno, the cardinal became extremely interested because here perhaps was the solution to a problem of his own. On the Albani estates at Soriano nel Cimino, to the north-east of Vetralla, was a shrine dedicated to the martyr, Sant'Eutizio. The cardinal's brother had been cured through the intercession of the saint and in gratitude had restored the church there and built a little monastery beside it. He had then invited a group of priests to live there, to take care of the church and attend to the spiritual needs of the local people. Unfortunately, the group of priests had broken up after a short time and there was now no one to care for the shrine of Sant'Eutizio. On hearing about the new Congregation of the Passion, Cardinal Alessandro Albani suggested to his brother that he invite them to establish a community at Soriano.

In the normal course of events there would then have followed a long series of negotiations, lasting a year or more before the foundation could be made, but in this case it was different because Cardinal Alessandro Albani's brother was no less than the

Vetralla. The chapel and hermitage on Monte Foligno

'*Camerlengo* of the Holy Roman Church', Cardinal Annibale Albani. As *Camerlengo*, he was 'the most influential member of the Apostolic Chamber and the *Economica* [the council of finances], making him a triple minister of finance, of agriculture, and of commerce and public works.'[20]

Cardinal Annibale Albani was delighted with the solution outlined by his brother. When Paul came to Rome at the end of November, it is probable that they met to discuss it. When he had secured Paul's agreement, the *Camerlengo* made all necessary arrangements. He had the pope authorise the Secretary of State, Cardinal Valenti, to write to the local bishop and to the Governor of Soriano instructing them to cooperate in the foundation. Paul thought it would be difficult to set up two new communities simultaneously as there were not sufficient religious, but the cardinal had a solution, as we learn from a letter Paul wrote to Garagni on 16 February:

The concern that the most Eminent and Reverend Lord Cardinal Albani of San Clemente had that I should go immediately to take possession of the shrine of Sant'Eutizio, in the district of Soriano, did not allow me to stay even two full days in Rome; and since as soon as I arrived in Soriano I began [preaching] a mission, which ended with great results, I have been unable to give you any more information about us, because of all I had to do. Now that I find myself at Vetralla with my companion, having arrived here yesterday evening, I want to let you know that the aforementioned cardinal obtained permission from His Holiness not only to admit twelve religious to profession, with a dispensation from some months of the noviciate to be given at my discretion, but also to have a number of religious ordained with the title of poverty.[21]

So it was that Paul would have enough religious for both Vetralla and Soriano. Toscanella would have to wait; he had gone to look at the place on his way back from the mission at Soriano and discovered that it was far from ready yet. If the people wanted a community to come from Monte Argentario, they would have to give them proper accommodation in keeping with the Rule. He had a letter written to the governor saying that the foundation would not be

Lantern used by Paul when travelling at night

Paul's pocket-watch

made until after the summer as there was 'nothing ready there'.[22] Meanwhile, the final preparations at Vetralla were being made by John Baptist, whom Paul had left there when he passed through on his way back from the mission.

On the First Sunday of Lent, 1 March 1744, Paul received the profession of vows of eight novices, including Fr Marcaurelio, who was to become Rector of the new Retreat at Soriano before the week was out; Paul's sermon was based on the text 'Go you also into my vineyard'.[23] The next day he set out with Fr Marcaurelio, two other newly-professed priests, a few brothers and six students. The walk from Monte Argentario to Vetralla took four days. In a letter to Bishop Abbati of Viterbo, in whose diocese Vetralla was situated, Paul described how they arrived in the town on Thursday evening and were welcomed by the clergy and civic leaders, who brought them first to the collegiate church where the Archpriest of Vetralla preached a fervent sermon in which he spoke well of the new Congregation, after which they were given dinner at the mayor's house. Paul wrote:

It was most edifying to see the Canons and leading gentlemen [of the town] serving the religious at table, having wanted first to wash our feet, which would have brought tears from the eyes of the most hard-hearted of people. On the following morning, which was Friday, we went in procession from Vetralla to take possession of the new Retreat, which was handed over by the Magistrate, in the correct manner, with the document, etc. The Te Deum laudamus was intoned, and then the Prior Mancini gave a brief but very devout sermon, after which I sang the Mass. After Mass there was a procession with the Blessed Sacrament in the ciborium around the little piazza in front of the church. The Blessed Sacrament was then placed in the tabernacle, and the ceremony of taking possession was thus concluded.[24]

On 7 March Paul, Marcaurelio, the brothers and four students continued on towards Soriano. John Baptist was left as Rector of the new Retreat of St Michael the Archangel, at Vetralla, with two students and the other two newly-professed priests as his community.

The Collegiate Church at Vetralla

Vetralla. The refectory and kitchen of the hermitage of St Michael the Archangel

He would continue to reside there for the rest of his life, and Paul too would live there from 1746 until 1769. The distance from Vetralla to Soriano is not great, so Paul and his companions were able to walk there in a day, arriving in the town that evening.

The next morning a procession set out from the collegiate church in the town to the shrine of St Eutizio. Paul walked in front, carrying a cross which he had received from the local clergy; he was followed by the other religious and a large crowd of people. After a ceremony similar to that held at Vetralla, the new community took possession of the Retreat of Sant'Eutizio and its adjoining church, described by Paul as the most prayerful and beautiful shrine outside of Rome.[25]

The year 1744 had again been a time of growth for the Congregation, going from one to three communities, with the number of professed religious increasing from six to seventeen. Paul decided that the time had come to look for the solemn approbation of the Congregation. In November he went to Rome. The city was deserted because of the dangers and disruptions caused by the War of the Austrian Succession. However, his trusted helper, Monsignor Garagni, was there and he was able to arrange an audience for Paul with Pope Benedict XIV who by 19 December had already set up a commission of cardinals to examine the question and make another revision of the Rule.

Having stayed in Rome during the early days of the commission's work, Paul returned to Monte Argentario at the beginning of January 1745. On the way back, he caught a chill which caused severe pains in his kidneys and sides. He could not get as far as the Retreat of the Presentation and had to remain with the Grazi family at Orbetello. For five months he was unable to move from bed because of the pain.

Paul had travelled back from Rome with a new postulant, Don Tommaso Struzzieri. Struzzieri was thirty-eight years old and had been a priest for fifteen years. He had received his doctorate in law (*in utroque iure*) from the Sapienza University and since then had been engaged in preaching missions. He had first met Paul in Rome in the autumn of 1743 in the church of the Capuchin Nuns opposite Santa Maria ai Monti. He gave this account of their meeting:

As I went in, I saw a religious dressed in black at the foot of the church and another in the middle; both of them were kneeling. As I went past the one who was in the middle of the church, he turned round and stared at me. Then I said to myself, 'Could this perhaps be Father Paul?' After saying a few words to the sacristan, who was at the kneeler in the middle of the church, I headed for the sacristy.

This religious followed and caught up with me in the sacristy, I turned round and said to him: 'Are you Father Paul?' And he added: 'Are you Don Tommaso Struzzieri?' And with one voice we both said yes. Then we greeted one another and I experienced within myself such a special feeling for him, and in the same way Father Paul (as he told me afterwards) felt such great fondness for me arise within his own heart that during the short time that he remained in Rome we did not know what it was to be separated from one another. Indeed when we went together to lunch at Count Garagni's, they had to call us repeatedly to come to the table, as we much preferred talking to one another about God.[26]

St Paul of the Cross lived in this room at Vetralla for twenty-five years

As he was leaving Rome after their first meeting, Paul had invited Don Tommaso to join the new Congregation of the Passion. His friends tried to discourage him from accepting the invitation, but after about a year he made up his mind and contacted Paul about his decision. Arriving at Monte Argentario on 15 January 1745, he received the habit and began his noviciate on 12 February and made his religious profession on 16 April of the same year. The novice master, Father Fulgenzio, considered him sufficiently committed at that stage and, because of the pressing needs of the rapidly-growing Congregation, Paul allowed him to be professed early; he had not yet used up the twelve dispensations from the twelve-month noviciate secured for him by Cardinal Albani.

Throughout his five months of sickness at the beginning of 1745 Paul continued to worry about the revision of the Rule which was being done in Rome. The commission was composed of Cardinal Girolami, Prefect of the Congregation for Bishops and Regulars, Cardinal Gentili, former Secretary of the same Congregation, and Cardinal Besozzi, a Cistercian who was described by Benedict XIV as 'a religious of exemplary life'[27]. Paul hoped for support from Cardinal Crescenzi, who was highly thought of in Rome, and also from Cardinal Annibale Albani. The work of the commission dragged on through 1745. During the course of the year, news reached Paul that the cardinals were of the opinion that at least for the student houses there should be stable sources of income rather than total dependence on providence. Paul was upset by this and asked Cardinal Albani to use his influence with the members of the commission. In the meantime, Cardinal Girolami became ill and was replaced as head of the commission by the same Cardinal Albani. However, he was of the same mind as his predecessor with regard to the question of stable income. This, Paul believed, would constitute a fundamental change in the nature of the Congregation, altering what he considered to be one of the essential points of the Rule. On 8 September, when Albani was at Soriano, Paul went to see him to discuss the various questions raised by the commission, particularly the radical practice of religious poverty which he was seeking to conserve.

A letter from Cardinal Albani on 12 January 1746[28] encouraged Paul to go to Rome at the beginning of Lent. Before leaving Monte

Argentario, he welcomed a group of postulants, among whom was one who would become his confessor on the death of John Baptist, the future Fr Giammaria (Cioni) of St Ignatius the Martyr. Paul brought with him to Rome one of the students, Giovanni of St Raphael. At Sant'Andrea delle Fratte they were given rooms by the Minims, whose protector was Cardinal Albani. Their stay in Rome lasted two months; the days were spent going from one office or palace to another, trying to get results. Finally, on 31 March Paul wrote to Fr Fulgenzio:

Thanks be to God, on Monday of Passion week, the twenty-eighth of this month, the day on which the holy Gospel says 'If any one thirst, let him come to me and drink, etc.',[29] the Vicar of Jesus Christ put his own signature to the Brief confirming our holy Rule; he wrote 'Placet Prospero', which is the Holy Father's baptismal name.[30]

A number of little changes had been made in the text but, as Paul said, nothing essential had been touched; the section on poverty was unchanged. There was exemption from the jurisdiction of the bishop with regard to the internal running of the house for those Retreats which had twelve or more professed religious. Paul had hoped to have the Congregation approved as an order with solemn vows, instead of the simple vows which were taken by his religious at the time. This would have given a fuller exemption from episcopal control and more freedom with regard to ordinations to the priesthood. It would also have made it easier to found a community of contemplative nuns, an idea Paul had had for some years. Nevertheless, the Apostolic Brief was a big step forward and gave greater stability to the Congregation of the Passion.

From the beginning Paul had acted as head of the Congregation. The foundation of the two other houses and the solemn approval of the Rules and Constitutions made it necessary to hold a General Chapter at which the head of the Congregation would be elected. The head of the Congregation was to be known as the *Preposito* or 'Provost General'. It would not be possible to hold a General Chapter until April of the following year, so in May 1746 the three communities voted on who the Provost General should be; Paul was elected unanimously.

NOTES

1. *Reg. et Const.*, 8.
2. *Ibid.*, 2.
3. *Words*, 163.
4. *Storia*, I, 513.
5. *Ibid.*, I, 514.
6. *Lettere*, I, 338.
7. *Storia*, I, 545.
8. *Lettere*, V, 30.
9. *Processi*, I, 67.
10. *Lettere*, II, 212.
11. Is 9:1; Lk 1:79.
12. *Lettere*, II, 213.
13. *Storia*, I, 556f.
14. *Lettere*, II, 218.
15. *Storia*, I, 558.
16. *Lettere*, II, 272f.
17. *Ibid.*, II, 280.
18. *Ibid.*, I, 232.
19. *Storia*, I, 604, n.33.
20. Gross, Hanns, *Rome in the Age of Enlightenment*, Cambridge, University Press, 1990, 46.
21. *Lettere*, II, 241.
22. *Ibid.*, II, 528.
23. Mt 20:7.
24. *Lettere*, II, 349.
25. *Ibid.*, I, 494.
26. *Processi*, IV, 93f.
27. *Storia*, I, 652.
28. Text in *Acta C.P.* (1933), 163f.
29. Jn 7:37-38.
30. *Lettere*, II, 70.

Chapter Six
(1747 – 1765)

The years 1746 and 1747 saw another significant increase in the size of the congregation, with eighteen postulants being received. Extra rooms were added to the Retreats at Vetralla and Soriano, but for Paul it was clear that new foundations must be made. He took possession of the property at Toscanella in June 1746 but it would be another two years before a community was installed there. The possibility of founding a Retreat on the outskirts of Rome was considered a way of opening up a new sector for missionary activity. After looking first at Santa Bibiana, Paul turned his attention to the little church of San Tommaso in Formis, on the Coelian Hill behind the church of the *Navicella* where he had first met Benedict XIII more than twenty years ago. The next foundation, however, would be neither Rome nor Toscanella. It would be south of Rome, still in the Papal States but near the border with the Kingdom of Naples, at Ceccano.

On 4 June 1747 the town council of Ceccano gave its approval to a foundation being made by the Passionists, or 'Passionaries' as they were referred to by the mayor, at Santa Maria di Corniano, a church and hermitage a few miles out of the town. The church had been built after an apparition of Mary and the child Jesus to a shepherd in the twelfth century. The Benedictines from Monte Cassino had established a small community there, from which it came to be known locally as *la Badia*, but they later abandoned it. Recognising the poor state of the buildings, the mayor of Ceccano had, in his address to the council, said that the 'Passionaries' wished to build their new Retreat 'on the ruins of Santa Maria di Corniano'[1] .

Paul sent Fr Tommaso Struzzieri to Ceccano in October to begin the preparations for the foundation; as a companion he gave him his own brother Antonio. After making contact with the town council, the two religious began preaching a series of missions in the area near the *Badia*. Struzzieri wrote to Paul saying that there was still work to be done on the house and that he should not think of making the foundation until the new year. (Paul had hoped everything would be ready for the feast of the Presentation of Mary in November.)

The new community who would join Fr Tommaso at Ceccano set out from the Retreat of Sant'Eutizio at Soriano on 4 January 1748. Paul went with the group which consisted of one priest, two

The church of Santa Maria di Corniano, Ceccano

deacons, two subdeacons and two brothers. It took them over a week to reach their destination. The weather was very cold and for thirty miles they were walking in continuous rain. The group arrived in the town of Ceccano on 13 January and were warmly welcomed by Bishop Fabrizio Borgia and the local people.

The next morning at about 8.30 Paul and the nine other religious set out for the *Badia*. The weather had become steadily worse and by now it was snowing. They walked barefoot in procession, accompanied by the bishop, the clergy and most of the townspeople. Paul led the way, wearing a rope round his neck and a crown of thorns on his head, and carrying the cross. When they came within sight of the *Badia*, Paul wanted to turn back. The position of the house was such that in winter it was in the shade of the mountains behind and had direct sunlight for only a few hours each day. Paul later wrote to the bishop, 'When I saw the spot, a mountain fell on my heart and I realised that it was not a suitable place; indeed it seemed to me to be a tomb.'[2] In spite of his first reaction, he decided to go ahead to the church and celebrate Mass there, as he had planned. During the Mass he received such great consolation that after Mass he told the others that he would make the foundation and that great saints would live in that Retreat.

Paul and his companions going in procession to the Badia to found the Retreat

The Retreat of Ceccano as it is today

It was the foundation of Santa Maria di Corniano at Ceccano which was to provoke the first concerted attack of the mendicant orders on the Passionist Congregation. Before leaving Ceccano, Paul received the news that the proposed foundation at San Tommaso in Formis in Rome was in danger because the canons of St Peter's Basilica were claiming that the church was theirs and were refusing to give it up. A piece of good news arrived at the same time in the shape of a letter to Fr Tommaso Struzzieri from the Bishop of Terracina, asking if the Passionists were willing to make a foundation in his diocese. There had also been a letter from Cardinal Albani to Paul asking him to come to see him in Rome on his way back to Vetralla to discuss what they should do in the light of the failure of the Roman foundation.

In the garden at the Retreat of Ceccano

In Rome, as well as meeting Albani, Paul was able to have an audience with the pope who showed great interest in the foundation of the new Retreat at Ceccano. On his way out of the palace, Paul learned from one of his friends that a group of religious who were opposed to the foundation at Ceccano had also asked the pope for an audience. That evening he went to see Monsignor Nardini, who was Cardinal Colonna's secretary. In great secrecy the monsignor showed Paul a petition which the superior and members of the Chapter of the friary of San Bonaventura on the Palatine Hill wanted the Cardinal to present to the pope on their behalf. As Protector of the Reformed Friars Minor of St Bonaventure, Cardinal Colonna was their official 'friend at court'. Before leaving Rome, Paul wrote to Bishop Borgia of Ferentino telling him what was going on, but advising him not to let the people know for the present.

The petition delivered by Cardinal Colonna was passed on by Benedict XIV to the Congregation for Bishops and Regulars. However, the opposition did not stop there. In April the Capuchin community at Alatri sent a petition to the local bishop complaining about the 'Missionary Fathers of the Passion of Jesus Christ'. Meanwhile Paul was negotiating with Bishop Oldo of

Terracina about the proposed foundation there. When the bishop, who was a Carmelite, wrote to Paul about the opposition of the mendicant orders, who now included the Observant Franciscans and Discalced Augustinians, he replied: 'As far as I know, it is the Capuchins who have stirred up the others, but since I hope they are acting from good intentions, I look on them with particular affection as instruments of the Divine Will, in relation to which I see these events.'[3]

It was during this difficult year that Paul began reading the works of the German Dominican Johannes Tauler. He felt drawn to Tauler's teaching on interiority and found in his writings a confirmation of his own spiritual experience and a more precise language in which to express it. According to Fr Giammaria, Tauler's sermons, which he read in the Latin translation of Surius, were of great consolation to Paul in times of worry or sadness.[4]

On 24 July the Apostolic Chamber, the office in Rome responsible for the temporal administration of the Papal States, decreed that all building work in progress at the new Passionist foundations was to stop and what had already been built was to be demolished. The

The sermons of Johannes Tauler, Paul's favourite reading in his later years

text of the decree was read in public in the main square in Ceccano in the presence of the members of the town council; it was then nailed to the door of the parish church. Paul ordered the religious at Santa Maria di Corniano to leave Ceccano and return to Vetralla but the people would not let them go.

The Reformed Friars of St Bonaventure sent their most famous member, St Leonard of Port Maurice, to speak to the pope against the Passionists. He was a famous mission preacher and close friend of Benedict XIV; afterwards he regretted what he had done, but said that he was only obeying orders. The town councils of the places where there were Passionist houses wrote letters of protest to the pope; there was even a layman who had worked for the Capuchins for five years who sent a statement that in his experience they always had plenty of the best food and wine and were certainly not starving.

Paul decided that the first thing was to start a campaign of prayer among his own religious and other communities who were sympathetic to the new congregation. He also prepared documents defending the Passionists with the help of Tommaso Struzzieri, whose legal training proved most useful, and sought the support of Cardinals Crescenzi and

The Franciscan Friary of San Bonaventura al Palatino

140

Community at prayer, Ceccano

Rezzonico. A commission of cardinals was set up to study the situation and in the meantime the demolition order was stopped. Finally, in April 1750, the commission gave a decision in favour of the Passionists who were now free to remain at Ceccano and to continue the work which had begun at Terracina and also at Paliano, south of Rome. On 2 May Paul wrote a circular letter to all the religious, now more than sixty in number, in preparation for the feast of Pentecost, in which he recalled for them some of the essentials of their way of life and invited them to pray with him that the Holy Spirit would renew the congregation after the struggles it had been through. He wrote:

Together let us invoke the Holy Spirit, the Paraclete, the consoling Spirit, asking him to come and fill completely the interior house of our soul and our entire Congregation. Let us cry out to this Father of the Poor, this Giver of grace, this Light of hearts, asking him to grant us the true spirit of our Institute, which is the true apostolic spirit, rich in all the virtues. Let us pray him to open the spring of the living waters of his grace, so that all of us may drink from it abundantly. Then, all burning with love, aflame with charity, we will light this divine fire in the hearts of our poor neighbours, by means of the preaching of the most holy pains of our Crucified Love.[5]

At the height of the conflict with the mendicant orders, Benedict XIV had protested to the opponents of the Passionists: 'Do you wish to destroy what we ourselves have built?'[6] He had always remained a discrete supporter of Paul and his community; now that the question was settled, he invited Paul and Tommaso Struzzieri to preach the first Passionist mission in Rome for the close of the Holy Year 1750. The mission, which was held from 7 to 21 December in the church of San Giovanni dei Fiorentini, was attended by crowds of people, including a number of cardinals, and the pope himself

Rome. The Church of San Giovanni dei Fiorentini

came one day to listen to the preachers, in this way showing to everyone his esteem for the Congregation of the Passion.

Having settled the difficulties with the mendicant orders, Paul was able to devote himself after April 1750 to the work of preaching and the making of new foundations. The mission he preached at Camerino in the region of *Le Marche* in 1750 brought about the conversion of Orazio Rebecchini, a well-known bandit, who attended the mission with twelve fellow-gangsters. Paul obtained a free pardon for him so that he was able to return to his family. This was only one of many encounters he had during his missionary work with robbers, smugglers and other fugitives from the law whose lives were changed as a result of their meeting him.

Three foundations were made south of Rome in the 1750s: Terracina, Falvaterra and Paliano. At Terracina Bishop Gioacchino Oldo had begun the building of a new Retreat in 1748, following instructions written to him by Paul. The work had been interrupted during the conflict with the mendicants and, before the problem was resolved, the bishop died. The building materials which he had gathered for the Retreat were confiscated by the Canons of the Cathedral to pay for his funeral expenses. However, a mission preached there by Fr Tommaso Struzzieri in 1751 stimulated new enthusiasm for the project among the people of Terracina, who collected money to pay the Canons so that the building materials could be used.

The last foundation of the 1750s was made at Monte Cavo in the diocese of Frascati. When all Paul's attempts to establish a house in Rome had failed, he turned his attention to this former monastery of the Trinitarians which he had first thought about as a possible Passionist Retreat as early as 1742. The community was established on 19 March 1758 in very difficult conditions. Paul hoped to make some improvements on the building, but it was only in 1770 with money donated by the Bishop of Frascati, Henry Stuart, the Cardinal Duke of York, that he was able to do so.

The year 1758 saw the foundation of the eighth Passionist house, on Monte Cavo, and it also saw the death of the pope during whose pontificate seven of those eight Retreats had been established. On

144

3 May, feast of the Finding of the Holy Cross, Benedict XIV died. Perhaps the most respected pope of the century, he was described by his contemporary, Horace Walpole, as 'a priest without insolence or interest, a prince without favourites, a pope without nephews.'[7] In the conclave which followed, the most likely candidate was the Neapolitan Cardinal Spinelli but, when his election was opposed by the King of Naples, his votes were transferred to another leading member of the *Zelanti*, the reformist group within the college of cardinals who were opposed to the Church being ruled by political pressures. Thus it came about that on 6 July 1758 Carlo della Torre Rezzonico, Bishop of Padua and close friend of Paul of the Cross, was elected pope, taking the name Clement XIII.

As soon as Paul heard the news of the election, he set out for Rome with John Baptist to congratulate the new pope and to ask him to continue to remember the Congregation of the Passion. By 15 July Paul was already back at Vetralla and writing for prayers to the abbess of the Capuchin Nuns at Santa Fiora: 'I am occupied in one of the most important pieces of business I've had for many years, that is, the solemn establishment of our poor Congregation on the occasion of the election of the new Supreme Pontiff who, I hope, will be very favourable to us.'[8] The same day he wrote to the prioress of the Dominican Nuns of Valentano, also asking for prayers and explaining that what he was hoping for from the new pope was the establishment of the Passionists as an order with solemn vows.

During his short visit to Rome, Paul had been able to see Cardinal Crescenzi to whom he sent a petition for the pope on 22 July in which he asked for two things: solemn vows and a foundation in Rome. Crescenzi presented the request to the pope on Paul's behalf but, after the audience, wrote to inform him that these matters would not be settled easily and that it would be necessary for Paul to come to Rome if the difficulties involved were to be overcome. However, Paul was unable to return to Rome until the beginning of December, as he had to preach a retreat to religious followed by two parish retreats to celebrate the Jubilee for the election of the pope. But, as always, things moved slowly in Rome.

Clement XIII, still well-disposed towards the Congregation of the Passion and its founder, seemed willing to set up a commission of cardinals to examine the question of solemn vows. Fr Tommaso Struzzieri had an audience with him at Castelgandolfo the following June. He reported to Paul that the pope was very favourable to them. In a letter to Fr Giammaria Cioni, Paul said that the Holy Spirit was working in Pope Clement's heart 'to bring the work to completion'; he explained: 'he wants to set up a commission of four or five cardinals after his own mind, who will be favourable to us, and since for the present there are none at hand, he is waiting to appoint some, which, it seems, will happen soon. In this way he will have his own men, in order that the result which he greatly desires may be brought about successfully'.[9] Objections raised by the Court of Naples interfered with the nomination of new cardinals and caused Clement XIII to delay setting up the commission until 1760.

Meanwhile, Paul had been involved in negotiations with Cardinal Spinelli, the Prefect of the Congregation for the Propagation of the Faith, over the possibility of some Passionists being sent to foreign mission territories. The earliest texts of the Rule had made provision for such work being undertaken; the Latin text approved by Benedict XIV in 1746 reads:

If God the Supreme Good sends to the Congregation brothers sufficiently competent in doctrine to be considered capable of winning back heretics and calling unbelievers to Christian faith, then as soon as they are called upon to work for their salvation by the Supreme Pontiff or the Sacred Congregation for the Propagation of the Faith, they are to go wherever they are needed.[10]

The cardinal had two places in mind but in each case an alternative to the Passionists was proposed in Rome and accepted. The third mission was in what at that time was known as Mesopotamia, probably at Mossul in Kurdistan. This time the other cardinals at Propaganda Fide were willing to entrust to the Passionists their first foreign mission, but the unexpected death of three religious at Vetralla meant that Paul had no one suitable to send. The three were Fr Giovanni Tommaso, rector of the Retreat, Brother Francesco and Fr Francesco Antonio (Appiani), who as a young man had first met Paul on the island of Elba in 1735 and who had been his secretary for a number of years. They died in December 1759 as a result of drinking wine from a barrel made from wood which had been treated with a poisonous substance. At the time of this tragedy, Paul was staying at Toscanella for Christmas, as he was in the middle of a series of missions in the Diocese of Montefiascone. Fr Francesco Antonio was forty years old and Paul had been his spiritual director for the past fourteen years. In a letter written six days after his death, Paul told Tommaso Fossi that the news had 'carried [his] heart away' but that he had gone through the experience in silence, as God had permitted it.[11] A chronicler of the period noted the effect on the mission to Kurdistan:

The unexpected death of several members of the Congregation, one after the other, placed an obstacle in the way of this good and holy enterprise and stopped in their tracks the good intentions and lively zeal of Fr Paul of the Cross. This unexpected and tragic accident obliged him to change his plans, or rather to postpone them until a better opportunity would arise.[12]

Fr Francesco Antonio (Appiani)

Another opportunity did not arise during Paul's lifetime; shortly after his death, a mission to Peking was blocked by the French Ambassador, who did not want Italian missionaries going there. It was in 1782, seven years after his death, that the first foreign missionaries of the Congregation were sent to Bulgaria.

The commission called for by Clement XIII to examine the question of solemn vows was finally set up on 24 February 1760. There were five members: Cardinals Portocarrero, Paolucci, Conti, Erba-Odescalchi and Cardinal Spinelli, who acted as chairman. Three of these (Portocarrero, Paolucci and Spinelli) had Passionist Retreats in their dioceses; the other two had been made cardinals by Pope Clement in September 1759.

Three sets of papers were prepared for presentation to the commission. The first was a collection of letters of attestation from fifteen bishops, four of whom were cardinals (two being members of the commission), in which they spoke of the great work done by the Congregation, particularly in teaching meditation on the Passion, and of the admirable way of life led in the retreats, in poverty, prayer and fasting. The second had been compiled by Fr Tommaso Struzzieri and was an attempt to justify the request by showing historical precedents. He gave examples of fifteen religious orders which had been granted solemn vows when less well established than the Congregation of the Passion. In case the cardinals might object to the name of the Congregation, he also listed twelve religious orders which had been approved with a title referring to some mystery of the life of Christ, or to Mary or one of the saints. The third text was the actual petition for solemn vows, which Clement XIII had suggested should be signed by all the members of the Congregation. A few had not signed it, but almost all had been willing and able to do so.

Having examined the documents, the commission met for the last time on 23 November 1760. They had asked Paul to be available to answer questions during the meeting. He sat outside the meeting room with his companion, Brother Giacomo of St Aloysius. Twice in the course of the morning he was called in to reply to the cardinals' requests for clarification on certain points of the Rule. By the end of the morning the commission members had reached their decision: nothing was to be changed for the time being. All five seem to have wanted to grant the petition but felt unable to do so for two reasons. The first of these was the extreme austerity of the Rule, particularly in relation to poverty. The commission thought that at least the student houses should possess an income, but Paul, as before, was not to be moved on this point and told them that he would prefer to see the petition turned down 'rather than remove this strong wall of holy poverty'.[13] The other reason came as a complete surprise to Paul: some of his own religious had written to the commission asking that the petition be turned down.

Paul had not suspected that there was opposition to taking solemn vows within the Congregation of the Passion itself. This fourth set of papers, letters of appeal from certain Passionists who were opposed to the petition which they themselves had signed, played a decisive role. Paul's insistence crumbled before the shock of realising that he had been deceived. Had his enthusiasm been so great that those who disagreed with him felt unable to tell him? Whatever the reason, it was a blow to him to realise that the greatest obstacle was the lack of support from his own religious and that their objections had been submitted to the commission behind his back. He returned to Vetralla a disappointed man.

A week after receiving the decision of the commission, Paul wrote a circular letter to the whole Congregation in which he announced the refusal 'for the time being' of the petition. He reminded the religious of the prayers and Masses they had offered that God's will might be done in this affair. Paul had reflected on the outcome at the feet of the Crucified, asking the Father for the light of understanding, and had been given the knowledge that the decision of the cardinals to delay the granting of solemn vows was an act of the Providence of God. 'And do you know why?' he asked:

Because our Congregation has fallen from its first observance and fervour; that earlier fraternal charity is no longer resplendent (in it); there is no longer that blind obedience, that true holy humility: fervour is little less than extinguished as much by night as by day, there is a great triumph of laziness in the exercises prescribed by the Rules, there is the greatest tepidity in rising to praise God in choir by night and day, mental prayer is full of drowsiness and lack of attentiveness of mind, and there is little or no reverence for the presence of God. There is a noticeable absence of exterior decorum, which indicates a lack of faith and interior reverence...[14]

Paul saw the refusal of the petition as a call from God to interior renewal. In the letter he goes on to say that it is self-love and pride which destroy the love of solitude, silence, modesty and obedience; the way to recovery of these values is through recognition of one's own nothingness, which he calls 'the foundation stone of the other virtues'. When these values are strengthened, then, he says, the Congregation will be established as an order with solemn vows. The decision of the cardinals to refuse 'for the time being' is presented by Paul to the religious as an invitation to inner conversion:

Therefore, dearest [brothers], be renewed in spirit and put on the Lord Jesus Christ; and clothed in Jesus Christ, make true humility of heart resplendent in you, both internally and externally; practice true and exact obedience, real charity towards one another, meekness and patience, supporting one another, bearing one another's burdens[15] *with great charity and helping one another; ...have a great esteem for silence which is the golden key which guards the great treasury of virtues, and so as not to go on at greater length, I ask you to be most exact in the observance of every detail of the Rules...*[16]

*The novices' garden on
Monte Argentario*

Later, Paul came to realise the wisdom of the commission's decision and when he could have received solemn vows from Clement XIII's successor, he preferred, as he said, to leave the door open so that those who found the life too demanding would be at liberty to go elsewhere, rather than remain in the Congregation to their own detriment and that of others.

While 1761 began for Paul with the disappointment over the question of solemn vows still hanging over him, it saw the completion of a project which was dear to his heart: the opening of a second Retreat on Monte Argentario, dedicated to Saint Joseph and intended as the noviciate of the Congregation. Until now the noviciate had been at the Retreat of the Presentation but Paul was concerned that this was not a healthy location for young novices. The side of the mountain on which the Retreat was built was exposed to the sirocco. It also overlooked the stagnant waters of the lagoon at Orbetello, which was not opened up to the sea until the next century and which in the summer time was a breeding ground for mosquitoes; many of the novices would catch malaria, which Paul attributed to vapours coming off the lagoon. He had been advised by doctors to build a noviciate on the northern side of the mountain, above Porto Santo Stefano.

It was in November 1753, when conducting the visitation at the Retreat of the Presentation, that Paul had gone out walking on the hillside one day and selected the site for the new house. The next morning he brought the rector, Fr Fulgenzio, and the community to see it and traced out for them with his stick the rough outline of the new Retreat. On the following day he went down to Orbetello to look for support from Giovanni Francesco Sanchez and other benefactors and to ask the King's minister and *intendente generale*, Don Jose Ignacio de Masdeu, to support his request to King Charles III for the land he had chosen.

With Don Jose's encouragement, Paul then wrote to the king, explaining his reasons for wanting to build 'a few cells for novices' and asking him to give 'a piece of uncultivated land near the Retreat [of the Presentation] for the building of these cells...'[17] Within two weeks of Paul's letter being sent, the Secretariat of State of the Court of Naples had granted the request made by 'Father Paul of the Cross, Provost General of the Congregation of the Passion of Monte Argentario'.[18] The attitude of Charles III and his court to Paul of the Cross was consistently benevolent, and in striking contrast to his refusal the previous year to recognise as a religious order the Redemptorists, founded by the Neapolitan, St Alphonsus de Liguori.[19]

Paul had also to write to the Abbot of Tre Fontane, Cardinal Prospero Sciarra Colonna, for permission to build the new house. He explained to the cardinal that, as well as providing a healthier location for the novices, this would leave ten or twelve empty rooms at the Retreat of the Presentation which could be used for retreats by clergy and lay people.[20] The cardinal not only gave permission for the building to go ahead but offered to contribute to the cost of the work, hoping that when it was complete, he would be able to 'send many more people to make the spiritual exercises'.[21]

The work of building the new Retreat was done by the brothers of the Congregation who were skilled in stonework, carpentry and ironwork; the priests of the community worked alongside them as labourers, carrying the materials. Work was slow and was hampered by lack of funds, in spite of the heroic efforts to collect money and materials made by Brother Giuseppino. A further setback was caused by the death on 16 April 1755 of Fr Fulgenzio who, as rector and master of novices, had personally directed the whole project from its beginning. The first companion of Paul after his brother John Baptist, he was esteemed by the founder as a saint and had spent most of his religious life as novice master on Monte Argentario.

In July 1761, almost eight years after the site had been chosen, the new noviciate was opened. Following the design given by Paul, the building was four sided, with a doorway on the north side opening out towards the sea. The chapel, on the south side, was entered from the inner courtyard, with the cells built around it on the other three sides. The well in the centre of the courtyard recalls the symbolism of the *Interior Castle* of St Teresa, while the whole structure is built in such a way as to centre the lives of the novices on the presence of God within. Paul's first visit to the new Retreat was in March 1762. On this occasion he wrote:

Br Giuseppino (Pitruzello)

*The Noviciate of San Giuseppe
on Monte Argentario*

This Retreat has been founded to serve as a noviciate and to be a seedbed of saints to provide the Congregation with stalwart and competent men, who will be intimately united with God by charity, to work for the salvation of souls by being resounding trumpets of the Holy Spirit, to proclaim to all the sufferings of Jesus Christ – the most efficacious means for the destruction of sin – and to urge souls to perfection.[22]

In December 1764 Fr Tommaso Struzzieri was made a bishop. Four years earlier he had been sent to Corsica by the pope to assist Bishop De Angelis in his work as Apostolic Visitor. Paul had seen this as a temporary appointment and had asked Struzzieri to continue to act as Procurator General of the Congregation. Father Tommaso's appointment as bishop, while it was an honour to the little Congregation and of service to the Church, meant the loss of one of Paul's most capable and trusted advisors.

A far greater loss struck him the following year with the death of his brother John Baptist. He had been Paul's most faithful companion from his earliest days. He had been elected General Consultor at the first General Chapter in 1747, a role he had fulfilled ever since. For many years he had also been Paul's confessor and spiritual director. Traditionally considered to be more austere and rigid than the founder himself, he was not, however, wanting in compassion. One of his companions, Fr Antonio of Calvary, left this testimony:

If he heard that any people were sick or in need, he would get bread or other food and go to help them with his own hands and console them; even when an old man, he would go two or three miles to give them help. He had the gift of tears and it seemed as if he had them for his daily fare; for this reason he would hide himself from people in order to give vent to his weeping, bringing the Bible with him to a place of solitude. As long as he lived, he never stopped studying and savouring the Bible.[23]

While he took his share of the work of parish missions, particularly in the early days of the Congregation, the ministry to which

*Monte Argentario
A cell in the noviciate*

he was most suited was that of preaching retreats to religious and priests. His great love of Scripture gave him a style as a retreat preacher which was both simple and direct, unlike the majority of preachers of his day. Like his brother, he had a practical common sense in his direction of others, as can be seen from what he wrote to a nun in difficulty:

With regard to the idea which came to you of transferring to another monastery because you see little observance in your own, I see that you wisely remark that we bring ourselves with us wherever we go and that we can find something to cause us suffering, something to struggle with everywhere. At present, my experience of monasteries of nuns is such that I do not know of one which is not in need of reform. So have courage and persevere; don't trust in yourself, but trust in God; and remain humble of heart. This is what is needed if we are to have good results in all situations and places.[24]

On 10 July 1765 John Baptist became ill with fever. The doctor who came from the town of Vetralla to see him said that he was in no danger and prescribed quinine. Paul, who knew his brother better, was convinced that he was dying. Weeks passed and John Baptist showed no signs of recovery. When Paul asked him how he felt, he replied, quoting Judas Maccabaeus, 'If our time has come, let us die bravely.'[25] His time did come on 30 August, with Paul at his side, after four days of raging fever during which he had lost consciousness and the power of speech three times.

Paul himself sang the funeral Mass, breaking down in tears when in the prayers he had to pronounce his brother's name. After the Mass, according to Fr Giammaria Cioni 'he said that he would never advise anyone to face such a risk and that he himself would never do such a thing again, for fear that it would break his heart with grief.'[26]

Monte Argentario.
The inner courtyard of the noviciate

NOTES

1. *Storia*, I, 685.
2. *Lettere*, V, 106.
3. *Ibid.*, II, 667.
4. *Processi*, I, 399.
5. *Lettere*, IV, 228.
6. *Annali*, 152.
7. J.N.D. Kelly, *The Oxford Dictionary of popes*, Oxford University Press, 1986, 298.
8. *Lettere*, V, 151.
9. *Ibid.*, III, 169.
10. *Reg. et Const.*, 10f.
11. *Lettere*, I, 710.
12. *Storia*, I, 1075, n.49.
13. *Processi*, III, 451.
14. *Lettere*, IV, 267.
15. Gal 6:2.
16. *Lettere*, IV, 268.
17. *Ibid.*, IV, 212f.
18. *Storia*, I, 1127.
19. Jones, Frederick M., *Alphonsus de Liguori – The Saint of Bourbon Naples*, Dublin, Gill and Macmillan, 1992, 231f.
20. *Lettere*, IV, 213f.
21. Giorgini, Fabiano, *History of the Passionists*, Teramo, Edizioni ECO, 1987, I, 172.
22. *Ibid.*, 174.
23. Cioni, Giovanni Maria [Fr Giammaria], *Vita del vero servo di Dio P. Giovanni Battista di S. Michele*, Tipografia Poliglotta Vaticana, 1934, 53.
24. *Ibid.*, 212.
25. *Ibid.*, 217; cf. 1 Mac 9:10.
26. *Ibid.*, 222.

Fr John Baptist (Danei),
brother of St Paul of the Cross

Chapter Seven
(1766 – 1769)

Rome. The church of San Tommaso in Formis
seen from the garden of Santi Giovanni e Paolo

One of Paul's aims which had not yet been realised was the establishment of a house of the Passionists in Rome. It had been his custom for a number of years to stay, while in Rome, with the Angeletti family, who were benefactors of the Congregation whom Paul had met at the time of the foundation at Ceccano. It was while staying with them on one of his visits to Rome that he had first met the Franciscan Cardinal Lorenzo Ganganelli, the future Pope Clement XIV.

Among possibilities tried for a Retreat of the Congregation in Rome had been San Tommaso in Formis, Santa Bibiana, San Saba and San Stefano Rotondo, but all of these had come to nothing. In 1766 Paul delegated his Consultor, Fr Giammaria, to find a little house with a garden which would be suitable as a residence for a small group of religious until the time would come when a suitable church and monastery could be found. With the help of the Angelettis and another good friend, Antonio Frattini, he discovered a suitable house in the Via San Giovanni in Laterano, between the Colosseum and the Basilica of St John Lateran, beside what is today the Irish College. It was the property of the Jesuit noviciate community at Sant'Andrea al Quirinale. Money was provided by Antonio Frattini, the Marchesa Muti-Sacchetti and other supporters of the Congregation, and the new Hospice of the Crucified was opened on 9 January 1767. Three months later, on 13 April, the oratory was blessed by Monsignor Giuseppe Garampi, who was Secretary of Ciphers under Clement XIII and favourable to Paul and his community.

Paul was now seventy-three years old. He decided to visit the Retreats south of Rome, while he was still able. In a letter to Antonio Frattini's sister, who was a Carmelite nun at Vetralla, he wrote:

In a few days time, God willing, I will be leaving for a last visit to our Retreats in Campagna and Marittima [the provinces south of Rome], as it is more than fourteen years since I have been there. I am going so as to embrace for the last time my brethren and sons, to whom I will also give a retreat to encourage them to be holy; then, if God gives me life, I will return here [to Sant'Angelo, Vetralla] to spend my last days. It is a long, hard journey, and I am a decrepit old man in poor health; I ask for your prayers.[1]

*The Colosseum,
looking towards the
Via San Giovanni in Laterano*

Most of the journey had to be done by carriage as Paul was no longer able to walk long distances. With Brother Bartolomeo, the infirmarian from Vetralla, as his companion, he went first to Monte Cavo in the Alban Hills and from there to the Retreat of Terracina, on the coast, where he stayed for some months because of the winter weather. He concluded his visit by giving the religious an eight-day series of meditations on the Passion of Christ. On 24 March he set out for the Retreat of Falvaterra, inland from Terracina and near the frontier with the Kingdom of Naples. All along the way there had been demonstrations of affection from the people of the region, who revered him as a saint. When he travelled from Falvaterra to Ceccano, where the people still recalled cures that had been

Antonio Frattini, friend and benefactor of the first Passionists in Rome

attributed to his blessing at the time of the foundation of the Retreat, the civil authorities had to provide an armed escort of soldiers because they feared someone would be crushed by the crowds of people who came forward to meet him anywhere he stopped on the way. The sick were brought out to line the streets as he passed by and people would tear pieces of his clothing to have a relic of 'the saint'. One woman tried to cut a piece of cloth from his habit as he stood talking; Paul asked her, 'What do you want that for? Are you going to make socks for the chickens?'[2] When he was leaving Ceccano to go on to Paliano, the last Retreat to be visited, Fr Giorgio gave him his mantle, because his own was by now cut to pieces.

On 6 May Paul arrived in Rome and went immediately to see the pope to thank him for granting permission for the opening of the new Hospice of the Crucified. He stayed at the Hospice to conduct the visitation; while he was there, Cardinals Pirelli and Ganganelli came to pay their respects, as did Fr Ricci, the General of the Jesuits. After a week in Rome Paul returned to Vetralla in a state of exhaustion. He became ill and was feared to be in danger of death. He received viaticum but, just when the end seemed near, began to recover. A long period of rest was prescribed.

163

Ceccano. A garden wall recalls the times
St Paul of the Cross visited the Retreat

In September 1767, Paul wrote to Fr Luigi Reali, a Jesuit at the Collegio Romano, to thank him for donating books to the Hospice at Rome. In the letter he expressed his anguish over the sufferings the Society of Jesus was enduring. He lamented the great loss to the Church resulting from the opposition to the Society but said that he believed that in God's own time, it would rise again to even greater splendour.[3] What Paul was referring to was the campaign for the suppression of the Jesuits being waged by the Bourbon monarchs, a campaign motivated by greed and a desire to lessen the influence of the papacy within their kingdoms. In the spring of that year, Charles III, the former King of Naples who had been King of Spain since 1759, had expelled the Jesuits and confiscated their property. Similar measures had already been taken by Portugal and France. These Catholic monarchs brought pressure to bear on Pope Clement XIII to approve what they had done, and in January 1769 placed before him an official request for the suppression of the Society, but the pope said that he would cut off his hand rather than sign such a decree. He called a special Consistory of Cardinals to formulate a reply. The Consistory was to meet on 3 February but, the night before, Pope Clement suffered a massive stroke and died.

Clement XIII had been Paul's friend and protector for thirty years. As Cardinal Rezzonico, he had worked hard to have the Rule approved and at the beginning of his Pontificate he had helped Paul in the attempt to obtain solemn vows. For the remainder of his pontificate, his energy had been sapped by the Jesuit question; he had been heroic in his defence of the Society. By nature indecisive and somewhat scrupulous, he had suffered greatly in his last years. He had always been favourable to Paul of the Cross, admitting him in audience at any time, but he had insisted that any requests made should be processed through the Roman Congregations, the departments or ministries of the papal government.

Copy of the Spiritual Exercises of St Ignatius given by the Collegio Romano to the community at the Hospice of the Cucified

Fr Giammaria wrote to Paul from Rome to inform him that Pope Clement was dead. Paul replied, 'I am greatly saddened by the death of the pope. This morning I offered Mass for the repose of his soul, and I prayed also that the Divine Mercy would provide a holy Pastor for his Church; I placed the hearts of the cardinals in the wounds of Jesus Christ, especially the heart of Ganganelli.'[4]

The conclave, which lasted three months, was dominated by the Jesuit question. Cardinal Pirelli wrote in his diary, 'If we make a mistake this time, the Church is in ruins.'[5] Meanwhile, Paul was in Vetralla preparing for the fifth General Chapter which opened there on 9 May. There were now twelve houses of the Congregation, a new Retreat having been opened at Corneto (known today as Tarquinia) six weeks earlier. Paul had hoped that he would be able to relinquish the post of Superior General but, in spite of his protests, the members of the Chapter re-elected him unanimously.

As soon as the Chapter was over, Paul had a new text of the Rule prepared, incorporating all the modifications made since the last papal approval. On 19 May Cardinal Lorenzo Ganganelli was elected pope, taking the name Clement XIV, in memory of his predecessor, who had made him a cardinal. Six days later Paul, who was now seventy-five years old, left for Rome. On his arrival, he was received affectionately by the new pope; he gave the pope a petition he had prepared asking for confirmation of the approval of the Rule.

Providentially, the pope lost the petition for, from the conversation they had had, Paul realised that the pope was willing to do whatever he could to help the Passionists. He prepared a new petition in which he asked for much more: he requested confirmation of the Rule with the changes which had been made, the approval of the Passionists as a Congregation with simple vows but having the same privileges as orders with solemn vows, the right to ordain members to the priesthood without special permission, and the right to collect donations in any diocese with the Bishop's consent (without having to seek the consent of the mendicant orders).

The pope gave the petition to Monsignor Garampi and Monsignor Francesco Saverio Zelada, Secretary of the Congregation of the Council and a friend of Garampi. They worked hand-in-hand

The Basilica of Santa Maria in Trastevere

with Paul and completed the examination of the Rule by 14 August. While the examination of the Rule was still going on, Paul had been asked by the Cardinal Vicar of Rome, Cardinal Colonna, to preach a mission in the city as part of the Jubilee celebration for the election of the new pope. Paul excused himself, saying that he was in poor health and that, besides, he was deaf. 'What matters is that the people who come to listen to you aren't deaf,' replied the cardinal; 'your voice sounds fine to me.'

Cardinal Colonna had suggested the church of San Carlo al Corso, but Paul thought it was too big and that, since he had not preached a mission for more than five years, he would be more suited to a smaller church. His preference was for Santa Maria della Consolazione, in the Campitelli district of the city; this tiny church near the river was frequented almost exclusively by poor shepherds, fishermen and domestic servants. Fr Giammaria noted that Paul chose it 'to be in the midst of the poor, who were always his most precious jewels.'[6] However, the cardinal anticipated a big crowd, so as a compromise, he assigned Paul to Santa Maria in Trastevere, which was a large church, but was frequented more by poor people than his original choice.

St Paul of the Cross preaching his last mission, in Santa Maria in Trastevere

Paul wrote to Brother Bartolomeo at Vetralla, asking him to post his sermons to him. The sermons were locked in a cupboard and Paul could not send the key by mail, so he told Bartolomeo to use his ingenuity to open it.[7] A few days before the mission was due to open, Paul had an attack of malaria. One of his companions had to replace him, as a high fever, accompanied by vomiting, kept him from taking part in the first days' exercises. Three days before the mission was to finish, he recovered sufficiently to preach. St Vincent Mary Strambi gave the following account of what happened:

As soon as he was able to mount the platform, he went to take part in the mission, moved by a strong desire to announce the truths of the faith to the people of Rome... There was a great crowd of people of every rank and class, including among them religious, secular priests, prelates, cardinals and the foremost nobles of Rome, and great was the fruit produced; because the venerable servant of God, with true apostolic freedom, without a shadow of human respect, and moved by zeal for the glory of God, inveighed vigorously against the vices and abuses which govern people. That huge audience could be seen in complete silence listening with full attention to the zealous missionary, and when he expressed his innermost feelings, especially in meditating on the Passion of Jesus Christ, they were filled with tenderness of heart. To tell the truth, it was enough to see the venerable old man, still recovering from his illness and so weak that, to climb the few steps to the platform, he needed the help of several people, some taking him by the hand and others lifting him under the arms; when he had reached the platform, he would stand up straight, leaning on his staff, his feet bare, his head uncovered. Then he would begin to preach, doing so with such liveliness, energy and power in his voice that it seemed as if there was nothing wrong with him, so strong was his desire for the salvation of souls.[8]

On the last day of the mission, 21 September, the crowd was so great that the piazza in front was filled with people who could not get in to the Basilica, and about two thousand more were turned away because there was no space for them in the piazza. Paul summed up the mission in a letter to Fr Giovanni Battista of

The Piazza of Santa Maria in Trastevere, which was filled to overflowing on the last day of the mission

St Vincent Ferrer: 'this poor, ignorant, rotting old man was listened to willingly by all and [his work] was blessed with results: Blessed be God.'[9]

The mission over, Paul was able to turn his attention once more to the petition he had made to the pope. Pope Clement had told him that everything he had asked for would be granted: the Congregation was to be approved by a Papal Bull. In October, Monsignor Garampi sent Paul a draft of the Bull for examination. He asked for a few changes to be made in the text, one of which shows his continuing concern for religious poverty; he wrote to Garampi:

I beg you... to remove the paragraph concerning the privilege of being able to receive donations, bequests or inheritance of stable goods which could then be sold. This privilege is contrary to the Rule, which prohibits us from accepting bequests of stable goods, and could obscure the strict poverty on which this Congregation has been founded and approved.[10]

Another point which he wished to have changed shows his concern for his religious. The commission had suggested that the superiors should be able to dismiss those who were no longer capable of living according to the Rule. While he agreed that those who were persistently negligent should be dismissed, he did not want the Superiors to be able to dismiss on the grounds of ill health or disability religious who had made perpetual vows; this, he said, 'would not be in keeping with Christian charity, since they had served the Congregation when they were able to do so.'[11]

On 29 October Paul went with Fr Giammaria to welcome the pope back to Rome after a visit to Castelgandolfo. Pope Clement brought him into his own bedroom. It was, said Paul in a letter to Fr Giovanni Battista, 'the room of a poor religious, with a poor bed, two chairs, a crucifix, a picture of Mary most holy, one of St Francis, and another of St Joseph of Cupertino. The walls are bare and whitewashed and there is not even the minimum of furniture.'[12] The pope gave him the final text of the Bull and said that he should take it to the cardinal in charge to have it copied out on parchment and the lead seal (the *Bulla* from which the document takes its name) fixed

Pope Clement XIV

to it; he told him not to worry about the cost, as there would be no charge made for the document.

The Bull, *Supremi Apostolatus*, was signed on 16 November 1769. The Passionists were now recognised as a Congregation of Pontifical Right, exempt from the jurisdiction of local bishops. The document made legal history as it was the first time that a Congregation with simple vows was given all the rights and privileges of orders with solemn vows. Paul had wanted the stability and apostolic freedom of an order, without taking solemn vows, as this would have necessitated mitigations in the Rule regarding poverty and penance. Clement XIV provided a solution by creating a new category of religious community in which to place the Congregation. Paul's community had started as the 'Poor of Jesus'; now they were known as the 'Discalced Clerics of the most holy Cross and Passion of our Lord Jesus Christ': over the years the title had been modified, but the community's way of life and its mission in the Church were still the same.

NOTES

1. *Lettere*, III, 686.
2. *Storia*, I, 1199, n.19.
3. *Lettere*, IV, 21.
4. *Processi*, I, 77.
5. Chadwick, *op. cit.*, 264.
6. *Annali*, 248.
7. *Lettere*, III, 294.
8. *Vita*, 149.
9. *Lettere*, III, 709.
10. *Ibid.*, III, 729.
11. *Ibid.*
12. *Ibid.*, III, 713.

The Bull 'Supremi Apostolatus'

Chapter Eight
(1770 – 1775)

When Paul had come to Rome in May 1769, it had been with the intention of going back to Vetralla when the examination of the Rule would be complete. At an audience with Pope Clement after the mission at Santa Maria in Trastevere, when he expressed his longing to return to the solitude of Sant'Angelo, the pope said that he preferred Paul to remain in Rome: 'I know what you will do in your Retreat of Sant'Angelo: you will pray for yourself, for us and for the whole Church. But you can do that just as well in Rome, and more besides.'[1] Pope Clement also promised to find a monastery with a church which would be suitable as a Passionist Retreat in Rome.[2]

Having seen his communities south of Rome, Paul wanted to visit the Retreats in the north. When it seemed that the worst of the winter was over, he went to see the pope on 19 March 1770 to say that he was going away on visitation. He took the opportunity of this audience to talk to Pope Clement about a project in which he had been engaged for some years and which was nearing completion: the founding of a monastery of contemplative Passionist nuns.

This idea had first come to Paul about thirty-five years earlier through his contact with Agnes Grazi and the Poor Clare Sister Maria Cherubina Bresciani, both of whom had hoped to become members of a female Passionist community. Paul shared his hopes for this foundation with some of those he directed, including Lucia Burlini, a young woman who had provided food for the Passionist community at Toscanella during the hardships of the early days there. Lucia was asked by Paul to pray for inspiration regarding the founding of the Passionist nuns. She sent him an account of what came to her as she prayed:

I asked the Lord to let me know somehow if the new monastery for women would be set up; in that moment I seemed to find myself on Calvary where I saw [my] crucified Love, and at the foot of the Cross a multitude of souls who were weeping, like doves, for their dead Spouse.[3]

Although building work on a nuns' monastery had begun at Tarquinia in 1759, Paul had delayed the foundation because he believed that it would not be possible until the men's Congregation was solemnly approved by the Church. With the publication of *Supremi Apostolatus*, he felt that the time had come to ask the pope to approve a Rule for contemplative nuns and grant permission for the opening of the monastery. Pope Clement was very pleased with the idea and promised to approve the nuns' Rule.

Paul left Rome on 27 March, accompanied by Fr Giammaria. The weather was still very cold and heavy rains had made the roads muddy. They travelled in a two-wheeled cart, staying the night at Civitavecchia and arriving at Tarquinia on the twenty-ninth. Before making his first visit to the new Passionist Retreat, Paul went to inspect the work done on the nuns' monastery. He was met by Domenico Costantini, who was paying for the building of the monastery in memory of his younger brother, Arcangelo, who had been murdered during a burglary of their home in 1754. Three of Domenico's sisters were Benedictine nuns in the town; one of them, Maria Crocifissa, had been directed by Paul for many years and had been chosen by him as the future leader of the first female Passionist community. He had written to her in 1766: 'If God lets me live to see the foundation, you can be sure that you will be the first woman to be clothed in the habit of the most holy Passion.'[4] Paul was pleased with the progress which had been made on the building, which was nearing completion. From there he went on to the Retreat of Our Mother of Sorrows, outside the town, where he stayed until after Easter.

Because of the bad condition of the roads, Paul and Giammaria decided to go from Tarquinia to Orbetello by boat, but a storm drove them back to land at nearby Montalto and they were obliged to continue on horseback. They covered the twenty-five miles from Montalto to Orbetello in driving rain, reaching the gate of the town just before it was closed for the night. The French officer in charge of the gate refused them entry, thinking that they were Jesuits who had been expelled from Naples. Fortunately, another traveller, arriving at the same time, recognised Paul and explained who he was. When his presence was made known to the officials in Orbetello,

The gates of Orbetello

they turned out to give him a hero's welcome. They pressed him to stay there and not to continue on to Monte Argentario until the weather would improve.

Two days later, when the rain had stopped, Paul and Giammaria crossed the lagoon in a little boat and climbed the mountain to the Retreat of the Presentation. They stayed two weeks on Monte Argentario, spending time both at the Presentation and at the noviciate Retreat of St Joseph. However, his visitation had to be cut short on account of a letter he received from Rome, asking him to return at once. He appointed Fr Giammaria to conduct the visitation of the other Retreats at Toscanella, Vetralla and Soriano on his behalf and went back to Rome, with Brother Francesco as his companion, arriving on 8 May.

Fr Giammaria (Cioni)

During the summer months Paul was busy with the text of the Rule for the Passionist Nuns. The pope appointed a Franciscan theologian, Fr Francesco Angelo Pastrovich, and Monsignor Zelada to examine it. The sections of the Rule dealing with lifestyle and spirituality were largely based on the men's Rule, while the parts dealing with the organisation of the monastery and the vow of enclosure were dependent on the Constitutions of the Order of the Visitation, founded by St Francis de Sales. Like the priests and brothers, the sisters were to take the vow to promote the memory of the Passion of Jesus. This they would do within the setting of their contemplative life, by offering women the possibility, at certain times of the year, of making retreats within the cloister and by teaching catechism to young women and instructing them on how to meditate on the Passion. The examiners wanted to take these points out of the Rule, as they seemed somewhat unconventional for contemplative nuns, but Paul would not agree to their being removed as he saw them as expressions of the specific nature of the Congregation.

The Rule for the Passionist nuns was approved on 30 September 1770, but work on the new monastery would not be completed until the following spring. Meanwhile Paul was struck by a severe attack of fever which brought him close to death. For two months he was hanging on to life by the merest thread. Then, when the end seemed certain and he had received the Last Sacraments, Clement XIV sent word with Brother Bartolomeo: 'We don't want Fr Paul to die yet.' When he was given the message, Paul was heard to pray, 'Lord, I want to be an obedient son; your Vicar has told me to ask you to lengthen my life a little.'[5] From that moment, he began to recover.

Among those in Rome who had heard about Paul's plans for the new Congregation of Passionist nuns was the Princess Anna Maria Colonna-Barberini. She was a rich widow and very religious. With the encouragement of her confessor, she thought of entering the monastery at Tarquinia and wrote to the pope for advice. Perhaps thinking that she might resolve the financial difficulties which were causing delays in the opening of the monastery, Pope Clement sent her an Apostolic Brief in which he not only told her to enter the monastery but appointed her as superior. The princess was quite overcome by this as her idea had been to enter as a lay sister. However, when the time came for the opening of the monastery, she did not appear. The chapel was blessed in her absence, but the group of women who were to form the new community were unable to receive the black habit of the Passion as had been planned because their future superior was not there; she wanted more time to think before making a final decision. Paul requested the pope's permission to open the monastery without her; this was done on 3 May and the postulants were then able to receive the habit, but it was another two weeks before the princess arrived. Two weeks after her arrival, she wrote to the pope saying that she wished to leave the monastery as she had 'neither perfect health nor peace of heart'.[6] When he read the letter, Pope Clement commented, 'We never intended to kill anyone. Let her do as she wants.'[7] The princess left a week later, on 7 June 1771. The Passionist life was too severe for her, but she later entered the Franciscan monastery at Narni where she remained for twenty-five years, until her death.

A year later, on 20 May 1772, the community of Passionist nuns, which now had eleven members, including Maria Crocifissa's two sisters who had received permission from the pope to transfer from the Benedictines to the new community, made their religious profession, taking in addition to the usual vows of poverty, chastity, obedience and enclosure, the distinctive vow to promote the memory of the Passion taken by their Passionist brothers. After their profession, Pope Clement sent a letter to the sisters in which he prayed that the Passion of Jesus Christ would remain imprinted and graven on their hearts and minds, and asked that they would always pray for him and for 'the Church entrusted to [his] weakness'.[8] The letter was dated 25 July 1772.

Clement XIV was certainly in need of prayers. Less than two weeks earlier he had received in audience for the first time the new Spanish Ambassador to the Holy See, José Moniño, later known as the Count of Florida Blanca, described by the historian Ludwig Pastor as 'exceedingly crafty, clever, a past master in the art of deception, and outstandingly active in working for the destruction of the Jesuits.'[9] During the audience, Moniño raised the question of a papal suppression of the Society of Jesus; he told the pope: 'My king is a very pious prince. He honours the pope and loves your holiness personally, but after carefully considering the matter in question he is firmly resolved to carry it out.'[10] Cardinal de Bernis, the French ambassador, explained the gravity of the situation in a report he sent to Paris on 21 July: 'It is a matter of a very serious nature for the pope if Spain is determined to view it in this light, especially if, as Moniño made me realize, the settlement of all the other matters which are so important for the Holy See are to depend on the outcome of the Jesuit question.'[11]

Until now, the pope appeared to have been playing for time, humiliating the Jesuits in public, while actually doing nothing to bring about the suppression. The pressure brought against him by the governments of Spain, Portugal, France and Naples was so great that it seemed only a matter of time before he would have to agree. Yet such a decision was not going to be easy, even if Clement realised that he could not escape it. A combination of threats and bribery from the Spanish ambassador won over those members of his staff whom he trusted most, but almost all the cardinals in Rome were opposed to the suppression. When, at the end of their first meeting, the pope was asked by Moniño for a regular weekly audience on a fixed day, he excused himself, saying that he would be unable to receive anyone as he was undergoing treatment for a skin complaint for the next three weeks, and then rolling up his sleeve to show the ambassador his arm. The difficult decision which lay before him was destroying the pope's health; depressed and plagued by insomnia as he was, the rash was probably aggravated by the stress under which he was living.

Six weeks later, on 23 August 1772, Moniño was admitted for his second audience. Pope Clement put forward a plan to bring about the extinction of the Jesuits without actually suppressing the Society; he proposed that they should be forbidden to receive novices, that the permission to preach and hear confessions should be withdrawn from them, and that the General's powers should be transferred to the Provincials. In this way, their colleges and missions would not need to be closed and the Society would eventually die out. However, this half-way solution was not acceptable to the ambassador who, at their third meeting, on 30 August, offered to submit to the pope a plan for suppressing the Jesuits. In the report on the meeting he sent to Madrid, Moniño wrote:

I drew forth a paper on which were written my intentions and views and I was about to read it when the Holy Father gently signed to me to desist. I put my paper away again but showed by my demeanour my displeasure with this refusal. The pope then said that he intended to undertake something which the other princes would be unable to oppose and with which His Majesty would be highly satisfied, but it would take time. My reply was that such a delay would expose him to many dangers and that only the complete suppression of the Jesuit Order would satisfy the king. I had to tell him clearly that if the delay was at all long a big fire might spring up, bigger than one thought – I meant the suppression of all the orders.[12]

After further meetings with Moniño and the French ambassador, Cardinal de Bernis, the pope accepted a detailed proposal for the text of a Bull of Suppression. In December he gave the text to Monsignor Zelada and told him to work on the final text with Moniño, making him swear an oath not to tell anyone what he was doing. On 31 December Moniño wrote to Madrid: 'Zelada has examined my draft for the Bull of Suppression, has approved of it, and praises it beyond all measure. He suggested only four unimportant alterations, to which I immediately assented.'[13] In spite of this progress, the pope still delayed the signing of the Bull and in order to gain more support within the Curia before doing so, appointed a number of new cardinals, including Zelada on 19 April 1773 and Giovanni Braschi, the future Pius VI, a week later. Twelve other cardinals were chosen with Braschi, but the pope kept the names of eleven of these *in pectore*, that is, in the secrecy of his own heart.

It was not until June that Pope Clement finally signed *Dominus ac Redemptor*, the document of suppression; he had decided that it should be merely an Apostolic Brief, not a Bull. It was dated 21 July 1773 but would not be published until 16 August. Moniño saw to the printing of it himself as he believed that the Apostolic Chamber could not be trusted. The text signed by Clement said that the peace

Castel Sant'Angelo

184

of the Church could not be assured if the Society of Jesus were to continue to exist; therefore 'after mature and informed consideration, and in the fullness of power which we have received from the Apostle, we dissolve, suppress, extinguish and abolish the said Society.'[14] The General of the Jesuits, Fr Ricci, was placed under house arrest in the English College. After a year he was transferred to the prison of Castel Sant'Angelo. Here he was not allowed to write or receive letters and the windows of his room were boarded up to prevent him having any contact with the outside world. He was forbidden to celebrate Mass and was taken to Mass on Sundays with an armed escort. Within two weeks of his arrival his food allowance was halved. When winter came, he was not allowed a fire in his cell. All of this was done on the instructions of Monsignor Alfani, a member of the special Congregation, or commission, which

the pope had set up to carry out the act of suppression. After being held in these conditions for two years, Ricci died in Castel Sant' Angelo, while his release was being negotiated.

With the suppression of the Jesuits, their houses in Rome were emptied of their communities and other religious orders were asked to take over their churches: the Capuchins went to the Gesù and the Conventual Franciscans to Sant'Ignazio. Before the suppression, Paul had suggested to Pope Clement that, in the event of the Jesuits being suppressed, their novitiate house of Sant'Andrea al Quirinale could be given to the Passionists. Paul was familiar with the house, which was directly opposite the papal palace, as he had

The Basilica of Santi Giovanni e Paolo on the Coelian Hill (centre)

made his retreat for subdiaconate there. The pope was pleased with the suggestion and said that he had been thinking the same himself. However, after the setting up of the commission for the carrying out of the act of suppression, on 9 August 1773, one of the commission members (probably Cardinal Zelada) suggested that Paul should ask the pope for the church and monastery of Santi Giovanni e Paolo on the Coelian Hill, allowing the Vincentians who were living there to move to Sant'Andrea. Santi Giovanni e Paolo was at that time away from the centre of Rome; Paul wrote to Pope Clement that it was 'more in conformity with the spirit of our Institute, being in a more solitary place.' In addition, the church and house at the Quirinale were smaller and would not, he said, allow the religious to carry out their life of prayer according to the Rule.[15] That some people in Rome were opposed to the Passionists being given Santi Giovanni e Paolo is clear from Paul's letter to the pope: they were saying that the new Congregation was too few in number to take charge of such a large, historic property and that these were backwoodsmen who would not take proper care of the church. Paul told the pope that he already had a group of thirty priests, brothers and students ready to move into Santi Giovanni e Paolo as soon as the order would be given.

On 23 August, a week after the publication of the Brief *Dominus ac Redemptor*, Paul was informed by Monsignor Alfani that the pope had approved the transfer of the Vincentians to Sant'Andrea and the giving of Santi Giovanni e Paolo to the Passionists. However, the Vincentians were not easily moved, in spite of being offered a house on the pope's doorstep and a church designed by Bernini, both of which were in better repair than the place they were leaving. They asked the commission for two thousand *scudi* to clear the debt they had incurred by having repairs done to the church and an annual income to help maintain the larger number of priests they would need in Rome if they were going to undertake some of the work which had previously been done by the Jesuits. According to Fr Giammaria, it was the older Vincentians who were reluctant to leave Santi Giovanni e Paolo; the younger men could not get out of it quickly enough.[16] Other religious orders, including Clement XIV's own Conventual Franciscans, already had their eye on Sant'Andrea al Quirinale; one group was said to be prepared to pay eighty thousand *scudi* for it.

The pope returned to Rome in October after his *villeggiatura*, the annual summer leave he took at Castelgandolfo, to find that the Vincentians were still at Santi Giovanni e Paolo. Rather than wait any longer, he decided to give Sant'Andrea to Paul. However, Cardinal Zelada's regular weekly visit to the Hospice of the Crucified was used by Paul to send an informal message to Pope Clement that he would rather wait for a house on the edge of the city than take one so near to the centre of things. The pope changed his mind and negotiations with the Vincentians were resumed, a conclusion which was acceptable to all parties being reached at the end of the month. Paul wrote to Pope Clement on 30 October, thanking him for the gift of a Retreat and church in Rome; he went on to say:

I rejoice in God that your Holiness has founded in this city, the Metropolis of the world, a house in which there will be a continual memory of the most holy Passion of our Divine Redeemer; this will be a perennial memorial to all Christians of the great piety and holy zeal with which your Holiness has always promoted in the hearts of the faithful the devout memory of the same Passion, so that it may be practised by them until the end of time.[17]

Five weeks later, the ceremony of taking possession of the new Retreat took place. The group of more than thirty religious who were to form the first community walked the short distance from the Hospice in the Via San Giovanni in Laterano. Cardinal Boschi, the Titular of the Basilica of Santi Giovanni e Paolo, sent his carriage for Paul, now almost eighty years of age. On their arrival, they went first to the altar of the Blessed Sacrament in the Basilica, where they sang the *Te Deum* in thanksgiving. From there they went to the house to begin their community life in what would be the last Retreat founded by Paul, celebrating Vespers together that evening and rising at midnight, as usual, for Matins.

Among the members of the community were Fr Giovanni Battista (Gorresio) of St Vincent Ferrer, who would succeed Paul as General, Fr Giammaria (Cioni) of St Ignatius, his confessor, and Fr

A courtyard in the Retreat of
Santi Giovanni e Paolo

Marcaurelio (Pastorelli) of the Blessed Sacrament, who was a year older than Paul and one of his earliest companions, and who would die in Santi Giovanni e Paolo the following March. There was also a class of nine theology students whose professor would be St Vincent Mary Strambi.

On 31 December 1773 Paul was taken by carriage to visit Clement XIV. There had been disturbances among the people on Christmas Day which continued until the first of January; these were brought on by discontentment with Clement's government, though he was inclined to blame Jesuit sympathisers. He was delighted to see Paul, whom he had not met face to face for a long time. He

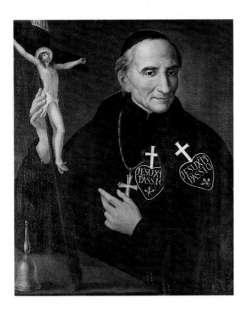

St Vincent Mary Strambi

received him privately, talking with him for an hour and three quarters, and when the time came for Paul to leave, the pope accompanied him as far as the door and then went out onto the gallery above the courtyard to watch him getting into the carriage.

Paul's last visit to the Quirinale was on 8 May 1774, when again the pope showed him signs of great affection, taking him by the arm into his own room where they spoke for two hours. These visits would have been of no small comfort to Pope Clement, who was still tortured by the Jesuit question. His mental and spiritual depression deepened, as he thought of what he had been forced to do. According to the ex-Jesuit Cordara,

The pope was haunted by the ghost of the dead Society of Jesus, again and again he remembered the damage its suppression had wrought on the Church, the dishonour his unfortunate decision had brought to his name, the hatred it had engendered... This distressing thought so racked him day and night that sometimes he would babble in sheer grief and seemed to be beside himself. Often in the night he thought he heard the bronze bell of the Jesuits, though no one had rung it.[18]

There were also a number of prophecies made against the pope's life which troubled him greatly. When, on the feast of Saints John and Paul, he came to venerate the relics of the two Roman martyrs and to greet the Passionist community in their new Retreat, he had another opportunity of speaking privately to Paul, this time in his cell, for about an hour. They discussed prophecies against the pope made by a woman from Valentano. Paul told Pope Clement to pay no heed to them and the pope left greatly consoled, for the time being.

During the summer months the pope became more and more concerned about his safety; an assassination attempt against the King of Naples increased his fears. He was afraid of being poisoned but, according to Moniño and de Bernis, 'the poison which was being administered to the pope by his enemies was the fear of being poisoned, which they were subtly increasing.'[19] They suggested to him that he should take no notice of such thoughts, but he continued to worry. Pastor writes that at this time Pope Clement 'ordered still more stringent measures of precaution to be taken. No one was allowed to enter the Papal palace with a stick; it was strictly forbidden to stand about in the courtyards; the Swiss Guards were doubled; and the two *Palafrenieri* of the night watch were picked out by the Pope himself.'[20]

Clement XIV was suffering from more than anxiety. His chronic skin complaint was now accompanied by mouth ulcers and it is probable that he had cancer of the stomach. His physical health deteriorated rapidly until, on 20 September, when he was in a high fever and suffering from an abdominal inflammation, he received the Eucharist as Viaticum. The same day, it was announced that public prayers were to be offered for the pope who was dying. When, on his deathbed, he was asked to give the names of those cardinals he had appointed *in pectore*, he refused to do so, adding, according to one source, 'that in his condition he could only look to the safety of his soul, which he had no desire to endanger any further.'[21] The next evening he received Extreme Unction, the anointing of the sick, and the following morning, 22 September 1774, he died. The only person with him was Fr Marzoni, the General of the Franciscans.

The rapid decomposition of the pope's body gave rise to rumours that he had indeed been poisoned, but these were discounted when it was learned that he had, before his death, had frequent visits from an Englishman called Menghin, who for two thousand *scudi* had sold him an antidote to poison, 'a powerful elixir which he had had brought from England.'[22] To put an end to the rumours, the Cardinal Camerlengo, who was Cardinal Rezzonico, nephew of Clement XIII, had an autopsy carried out and made the results public, together with reports from the doctors who had looked after the pope during his illness.

When Paul heard the news that Clement XIV was dead, he broke down in tears. He attended the Requiem Mass celebrated in the Basilica of Santi Giovanni e Paolo, after which he retired to his cell, asking to be left alone for the rest of the morning. Clement had been a true father to the Congregation of the Passion, but he had in his turn treated its founder as a father, turning to Paul for comfort and encouragement. He had given the Congregation that stability

Window of Paul's cell in Santi Giovanni e Paolo

in the Church which Paul had sought for many years, but his pontificate was marked by instability and turmoil. Remembered by the Passionists as the pope who helped them most, he is remembered by history as the pope who suppressed the Jesuits. In his *History of the Popes* Pastor described Clement XIV as 'one of the weakest and most unhappy of the long line of Popes, and yet one most deserving of sympathy, for though filled with the best intentions he failed in almost everything, being quite unfitted to deal with the extraordinarily difficult situation.'[23]

The conclave which followed the death of Clement XIV lasted one hundred and thirty-four days. A successor had to be found who was acceptable to both the pro-Jesuit and the anti-Jesuit cardinals. Finally, Cardinal Braschi, one of the two cardinals named by the late pope in his last consistory, was elected. Although a cardinal for less than two years, Braschi, who took the name Pius VI, had worked in the papal administration for over twenty years, having been private secretary to Benedict XIV from 1753 to 1758. Within two weeks of his election, the new pope visited Paul at Santi Giovanni e Paolo on 5 March 1775, being received in his cell by the old man, who was confined to bed. Paul told him: 'When your predecessor died, I wept because I felt like an orphan, but I am an orphan no longer; I have a father, and what a father!'[24]

Paul's life was almost over, but he had not yet finished his work as founder. He wished to undertake a thorough revision of the Rule which, with the approval of the general Chapter to be held that year, he would present to Pius VI for confirmation. At the beginning of March he started working on the text with the help of the rector of the Retreat, Fr Giuseppe Giacinto, who would read the text to him and then note his comments.

The Chapter opened on 15 May, after three days of prayer by all the capitulars. A special permission had already been granted by the pope to have Paul re-elected as General. He objected that he was too old and sick to continue but, in spite of his protests, he was elected unanimously at the first ballot. At the end of the Chapter, which closed on 20 May, the revised text of the Rule was presented to Pius VI with a request that he confirm the approval given in the Apostolic Brief of Benedict XIV and the Bull of Clement XIV.

Pope Pius VI

The pope entrusted the examination of the Rule to Cardinal Zelada and Cardinal delle Lanze who, as a boy, had first met Paul on the streets of Turin more than fifty years earlier. When their work was done, Pius VI confirmed the new text of the Rule by the Bull *Praeclara virtutum exempla*, which he signed on 15 September 1775.

It was towards the end of April 1775 that Paul met Rosa Calabrese, whose brother, a priest, was Cardinal Zelada's secretary. According to Rosa, who was a witness at Paul's Canonisation Processes, he had been sending her letters of spiritual direction since she was in her early twenties, about ten years before their first meeting. Rosa had come to Rome because of the Holy Year and was to stay for about two months, during which she had frequent meetings with Paul in the sacristy of Santi Giovanni e Paolo. Her accounts of their conversations give an insight into Paul's early prayer life, though at times the language she uses to describe his mystical experiences is at variance with the descriptions Paul himself has left us.

As the year progressed, Paul's health deteriorated. He celebrated Mass for the last time on the feast of Corpus Christi, 15 June 1775. After this, one of the priests of the community would celebrate Mass each day in the chapel adjoining his cell; Pope Pius VI gave him a dispensation from the Eucharistic fast, which at that time was from midnight, so that he would be able to receive communion with less difficulty.

On 29 August the doctor told him that he did not have long to live and that he should receive Viaticum. Paul asked that the whole community of the Retreat be informed that he would do so the next morning, so that they could all be present. On the morning of the thirtieth, all the religious walked in procession from the Basilica up the stairs to Paul's cell. They carried lighted candles, and behind them walked Fr Giovanni Battista, Paul's First Consultor, with the Blessed Sacrament. Those who were able gathered in his cell, while the others stood in the corridor outside. Before receiving the Eucharist, Paul addressed to them his last spiritual testament. He began:

Before anything else I recommend to your attention the observance of that most holy reminder given by Jesus Christ to his disciples:

Altar in the chapel beside Paul's cell

'By this all will know that you are my disciples, if you have love for one another'.[25] *This, dearest brothers, is what I desire with all the affection of my poor heart, both for you who are present and for all the others who are now wearing this habit of penance and mourning in memory of the Passion and Death of our most loveable divine Redeemer, and equally for all who, by God's mercy, will be called in the future to this little flock of Jesus Christ. In addition, I recommend to all, and especially to those who will hold the office of superior, that there should flourish more and more in the Congregation the spirit of prayer, the spirit of solitude and the spirit of poverty, and you can be sure that if these three things are maintained, the Congregation 'will shine like the sun'*[26] *in the sight of God and people.*

He went on to ask that special prayers be offered for Pope Pius VI, and that the community show special gratitude to Antonio Frattini for all that he had done to bring the Congregation to Rome, and to Doctor Giuliani, who had cared for Paul in his last illness. He also had a special word of thanks to Brother Bartolomeo, the infirmarian. He concluded by asking pardon of all the members of the Congregation for his failures as General and for any bad example he had given. Then he said in prayer, 'My dear Jesus..., I commend to you now and for ever the poor Congregation which is the fruit of your Cross, your Passion and your Death.'[27]

For more than six weeks Paul lay in his cell, unable to move, waiting for death. His confessor, Fr Giammaria, returned from the mission he had been preaching at Caprarola, near Viterbo, to be with him. Fr Tommaso Struzzieri, now Bishop of Amelia, wrote to say that he would come to see Paul and asking him to wait for him. 'Tell me what to write to him in reply; will you wait for him?' asked Fr Domenico, Paul's secretary. 'Yes, write to him that I'll wait', said Paul smiling.[28]

Just before midday on 18 October Bishop Struzzieri arrived. He went immediately to the dying man's room where Paul had been expecting him from one moment to the next. They talked for a while and then Paul asked Brother Bartolomeo to make sure that someone would take care of the bishop and see that he had something to eat as he was still one of the family.

*Death mask of
St Paul of the Cross*

In the middle of the afternoon, as Paul lay there quietly, with Brother Bartolomeo watching at his side, he suddenly turned towards the crucifix and then said to Bartolomeo, 'Tell Fr Giammaria to come to me so that he can be here when I die; my death is very near.'[29] The infirmarian did not want to disturb the community who were at Vespers, so he waited until the Office would be over and went to call Fr Giovanni Battista just as the community were leaving the church. The two of them went together to Paul's cell where Paul told them to call the community as he wanted them to be with him when he died. Fr Giovanni Battista tried to convince him that he was not dying, saying that he probably felt cold because of the change in the weather. Paul insisted that he was dying and asked him again to call the others. Brother Bartolomeo asked Fr Giovanni Battista to call at least Fr Giammaria and Bishop Struzzieri, but when he had gone out to do so, Bartolomeo noticed a change in Paul's condition which made him run out and summon the whole community. Someone went to tell Antonio Frattini who came at once with his son Vincenzo.

All those present joined in the prayers of commendation of the dying, which were led by the rector. Then Fr Giammaria gave him absolution, after which he received the Papal Blessing, which Pius VI had instructed Fr Giovanni Battista to impart at the moment of Paul's death. The rector then began to read the account of the Passion of Christ from the Gospel of St John. Bishop Struzzieri leaned over and whispered in Paul's ear: 'Fr Paul, when you get to heaven, remember the poor Congregation for which you have worked so hard, and remember all of us, your poor children.' Paul made a sign as if to say, 'Yes, I will.'[30] Then he closed his eyes as if he were sleeping and, after about fifteen minutes, he quietly breathed his last. It was about four forty-five in the afternoon.

Antonio Frattini went to give the news to the pope who, on hearing that Paul had died, said 'How lucky he is!'[31] Pope Pius ordered that he should be buried in a wooden coffin, enclosed in another one, made of lead, and placed in a tomb of his own, rather than being buried in the common burial place of the religious. He said that he himself would pay the expenses involved. The next morning, at six o'clock, Paul's remains were brought to the Basilica of Santi Giovanni e Paolo; the body was placed on a wooden board with a brick under the head for a pillow, as prescribed by the Rule.

A large crowd of people had been standing in the rain, waiting for the doors to be opened so that they could venerate the body of him whom they already referred to as 'a saint'.[32] Once the doors were opened, there were so many people trying to get close to the body that a barrier of planks had to be set up to keep the crowd at a safe distance. Inside the barrier, to keep order, stood the *Cavaliere* Giusto Franchesperg, a close friend of Paul from Trieste in Germany, and the ever-faithful Antonio Frattini with his son. When evening came, the basilica was closed and, before the body was moved to a side room near the entrance, the painter Gian Domenico Porta took a cast of the face for the death-mask. In the side room, the body was placed in a coffin of pine, which was enclosed in another of lead. When sealed, the lead coffin was placed in a third coffin made from chestnut. This was buried in a tomb which had been hurriedly cut out of the wall of the basilica near the main door, on the left-hand side. The Office of the Dead and Mass were celebrated in the basilica each day for seven days, the Mass on the last day being celebrated by Bishop Tommaso Struzzieri who afterwards said that he had the impression he was offering Mass for someone else, so strong was his conviction that Paul was already in heaven.[33]

Shortly after the funeral, Pope Pius VI asked the new General, Fr Giovanni Battista, to begin preparations for opening the Cause of Canonisation of Paul of the Cross. The first session of the Ordinary Processes was held at Rome on 7 January 1777, just fifteen months after Paul's death. In 1786 a biography was published, based on Paul's letters and on the testimony of the witnesses at the various Processes held at Rome, Vetralla, Corneto (Tarquinia), Orbetello, Gaeta and Alessandria. The author was St Vincent Mary Strambi who, as a member of the community of Santi Giovanni e Paolo, had been with Paul for the last two years of his life. The future bishop of Macerata and Tolentino wrote Paul's life-story on his knees in the cell at Vetralla where the Founder had lived for twenty-five years.

The room in which Paul died. The crucifix was used by him during his missions

St Paul of the Cross was canonised on 29 June 1867. Among those canonised that day was the Franciscan St Leonard of Port Maurice, whose superiors had told him to complain to Benedict XIV about Paul and his Congregation, after the foundation at Ceccano. On the same day the holiness of both was affirmed by the Church.

The community founded by Paul continued to grow and spread after his death. The way of life mapped out in the Rule has been confirmed as a path to holiness by the Beatification or Canonisation of about forty members of the Congregation; many others have been declared Venerable, including Paul's own brother, John Baptist, and some of his first companions. Today Passionists are to be found living out Paul's vision in more than fifty countries, seeking to respond to the challenges of our world in fidelity to Paul's founding inspiration and to bring freedom and life to those 'who do not experience the fruit of the Passion of Jesus'.[34]

I place my trust in God.
The Congregation is his;
the lights he gave me for founding it were his.
He will take care of its progress.
My hope is in God.

St Paul of the Cross[35]

Chapel of St Paul of the Cross
in the Basilica of Santi Giovanni e Paolo, Rome

NOTES

1. *Vita*, 150.
2. *Ibid.*
3. *Storia*, I, 1294f.
4. *Lettere*, II, 309.
5. *Processi*, I, 103.
6. Gaetan du S. Nom de Marie, *S. Paul de la Croix et la Fondation des Religieuses Passionistes*, Tirlemont, Soeurs Passionistes Missionnaires, 1936, 85.
7. *Ibid.*
8. *Vita*, 172.
9. Pastor, Ludwig, *The History of the Popes from the close of the Middle Ages*, London, Routledge and Kegan Paul, 1951, Vol. XXXVIII, 217.
10. *Ibid.*, 230.
11. *Ibid.*, 231f.
12. *Ibid.*, 234.
13. *Ibid.*, 250.
14. Chadwick, *op. cit.*, 374.
15. *Lettere*, IV, 205.
16. *Storia d. Fond.*, in *Bollettino* (1926), 110.
17. *Lettere*, IV, 206.
18. Cordara, *De suppressione S.J.*, 151f., quoted in Pastor, *op. cit.*, 525.
19. Pastor, *op. cit.*, 527.
20. *Ibid.*
21. Centomani to Tanucci (23 September 1774), quoted in Pastor, *op. cit.*, 532.
22. Centomani to Tanucci (4 October 1744), quoted in Pastor, *op. cit.*, 535, n. 1.
23. Pastor, *op. cit.*, 550.
24. *Processi*, IV, 215.
25. Jn 13:35.
26. Mt 13:43.
27. *Lettere*, V, 256-258.
28. *Processi*, IV, 77.
29. *Ibid.*, IV, 321.
30. *Ibid.*, IV, 323.
31. *Ibid.*, IV, 429.
32. *Ibid.*, IV, 324.
33. *Ibid.*, IV, 10.
34. *Words*, 22.
35. *Processi*, IV, 225.